Brussels
June 2014

Eastern Man, Western Man
Essay on the modelling of thought and action

Book 1
The Diamond of Knowledge

Eastern Man, Western Man
Essay on the modelling of thought and action
Book 1
The Diamond of Knowledge
Bijan Ghalamkaripour
June 2014
bijanghalamkaripour@yahoo.fr

© 2014 Bijan Ghalamkaripour
Published by Books on Demand,
12/14 rond-point des Champs-Elysées,
75008 Paris, France
Printed by Books on Demand GmbH, Norderstedt, Germany
Legal deposit: August 2014
ISBN: 978-2-322-03636-3

Bijan GHALAMKARIPOUR

Eastern Man, Western Man
Essay on the modelling of thought and action

Book 1
The Diamond of Knowledge

TABLE OF CONTENTS

Introduction

Modelling simplifies a subject, so that it is better understood by all. In this sense and since my early years, my motivation to study knowledge, ideology and action has enriched my thoughts: simplifying a subject can effectively permit everyone to better understand it. There are many reasons for me having this desire and this interest in researching origins was born a long time ago.

Coming from Iran, I have lived through major upheavals which rocked my country. Having experienced the Iranian revolution of 1979, I wanted to understand its roots; to understand the genesis of a revolution in a country without any major economic difficulties. It seemed that no existing theory could explain the foundations of the revolution. Thus, I wanted to adopt a different angle, one which I could make my own. I wanted to carry out an autopsy, to understand the causes and the means, whilst making comparative studies with other revolutions which had taken place at different places and times.

At the University of Tehran, as a student, I began the first official work, but always in a student environment. The topic was vast and interesting: what are the sociological causes of development and/or under-development of a country? Conducting research on the different expounded theories on this topic by 'social thinkers' I noticed how this question had intrigued and captivated many commentators. To understand the project of a society it is interesting to take a global view of the world and its history. From the Old Testament to the myths of China and India to Herodotus, Ibn Khaldoun and Montesquieu, many thinkers and sociologists have discussed the points of convergence and divergence of developed and under-developed countries.

After university, I was thus interested in and enthusiastic about the work of authors, whether Iranian or not, proposing theories about the intelligence or lack of intelligence of Iranians, on their 'madness', their objective and subjective understanding of life. For some 'essayists', the causes for the backwardness of third world countries, like Iran, were due to illiteracy rates. Not reading and not writing lead to ignorance about the modern world, therefore to the impossibility of being open to innovation, to development, and to having a rational view of things. If one wants to move towards modernity, one must open himself to the West and its ideals. In contrast, other thinkers push Iran to withdraw inwards so as to avoid westernisation and unbridled modernity. It was these ambivalences, these extremes which led me to this research; trying to distinguish as far as possible, truth from falsity, find the balancing point.

This essay is not meant to be pretentious and I hope that it will be addressed. One of the objectives of this work is to propose a theory, using a micro-explanation of individual behaviour and macro-research on the origins of historical changes, to bring in line two main themes of sociology: determinism and the school of understanding. My task is therefore to create a theoretical framework facilitating the study of divergences between the social values existing in the East and the West and thereby offering a clearer view of a founding theory such as 'the understanding and modelling of interactions', knowledge of the fundamental philosophical questions.

Concerning the title of this essay, namely 'Knowledge and Actions', I should clarify that knowledge is one of the most fundamental topics of discussion in philosophy. It is the founding stone of man's actions. Knowledge guides all our attitudes and our beliefs and it is for this reason that studying its workings can shed light on its various 'models', create a typology of different ideologies and as a consequence, of different types of action. Modelling, in its broad sense, is the abstract representation of a phenomenon in order to facilitate its study. This can help us in theorisation and finally in the construction of a descriptive and explanatory system.

What follows is, I think, a rather new and innovative discourse; even if it isn't exhaustive. And as is the case with anything new, it demands inquiry and analysis, meaning that I am not entirely certain of its veracity. I am therefore without pretention. If I publish it, it is because I am aware of its imperfection and await to confront it so as to enrich it. I would therefore be happy to receive critical comments.

It is with honour and gratitude as a husband that I thank my wife, for her great support, because, without her, I would not be able to complete this work. I would like to thank Mary Munroe for her work on the English translation of this book.

Bijan Ghalamkaripour
June 2014, Brussels, Belgium

bijanghalamkaripour@yahoo.fr

Knowledge and Action

The most basic, the most mundane of man's activity is action. It is the material or symbolic expression of a will to reach a goal. In collective life, individual behaviour is transformed into social action and thus inevitably, into social contacts, provoking a reaction. It is in this way that social interaction comes about.

From the moment of birth, humans are immersed in social actions. Man is never alone which is the reason for which we can say that he is not a psychological being, in the sense of being bent over a psychical monad which separates him from the world, but a social being in continuous interaction with his environment. This socialability is due to the existential need of man. Even if he is subjected to change during his lifetime, transformed by his experiences into an asocial or anti-social person. He is and he remains a social being. According to the majority of sociologists, the concept of social action is one of the most fundamental in sociology, because social action is not only the essential element in the life of man, even when man lives alone, but also - in view of the importance given to this concept - the subject of study in sociology, which can be the object of different interpretations and discussions.

During the 18th century, before sociology became a science in itself, the question of social action was considered in different works of social thinkers. However, in sociology, as a modern science, the discourse on social action is a pioneering discourse. On this basis, we can say that in sociology, the study of social interaction is divided into two main categories: determinism and 'reactionism'. Clearly, each of these categories has its own methods of analytical approach which compete and sometimes conflict. It is therefore interesting to understand the essential factor of the action of thinkers.

A - Determinism

Determinism is the explanation of individual behaviour by external causes, that is to say, by placing it in pre-established contexts. These patterns are derived from two sources: on one hand, a system of internalised norms, on the other hand, the hierarchical structure of different social positions. The theories of thinkers such as Saint Simon, Karl Marx and Émile Durkheim are to be found in this category. In the first half of the 19th century, Saint Simon effectively spoke of social action to explain the social aspect of what he called 'the science of history'. The new systems and major changes with which he was confronted, he referred to them as the 'industrial society'. According to him, the history of European societies took place at different phases: the theological phase, the military phase and finally the industrial phase. Auguste Comte, his secretary, took up the idea of these three phases and called them Theology, Metaphysics and Positivism. In the industrial society, all the social forces are at the service of human dignity. The future elites will come from the working class which is the most fundamental class of society and which is the nurturing class of this new society. Additionally, according to Saint Simon, the historical evolution began after the 1789 revolution, and the best members of society, that is to say, the scholars, labourers, the bankers and the industrialists form a unit of this class.

With this historic change "social organisations" began to change. The major events of this year taking place in Paris were: the occupation of the former prison, the taking of the Bastille on July 14, 1789, the Universal Declaration of Human Rights on 26 August 1789, the popular uprising in Paris on 5th and 6th October 1789, the nationalisation of the Catholic clergy etc... For Saint-Simon, one can recognise the difference between the Ancien Régime and the "industrial society" by the difference that characterises their actions. Action in the Ancien Régime, is essentially based on conflict, defense, military confrontation and war. Whilst in the industrial society, the new form of action is based on production and industrial development as well as creativity. Society then articulates its supremacy by progress and not by confrontation. In this new society, social classes are categorised by criteria concerning positive action: the productive class is the industrial class that positively produces and in concrete terms, is the only active class. 'Active', means here that which potentially has the power to create material and cultural goods. The opposite of this industrial class, is the noble class. With no active role, they were considered to be pests. To create a fertile ground for the emergence of an industrial society, one can only rely on the active class, made-up of labourers, industrialists, lawyers ... Every act done by an "active" is a social and political act to raise awareness of the importance of their situation. An active member of society has the power to act. The ultimate goal is to coordinate all activities into a harmonious set of productive actions.

Until 1870, Saint-Simonianism strongly influenced the emergence of "social" thinkers, based on two schools of thought: capitalism and socialism. The bourgeoisie, composed of bankers and patrons, viewed its economic activities as a social vector leading to industrial progress. What appeared was an acceleration of economic development leading to the emergence of a new society and individual freedoms. One discovers amazing divergences in the ideas of Saint Simon. He accorded great importance to the ability of engineers and technicians, but also to society. Social tradition considered Saint Simon to be the founder and the first theoretician of socialism.

Proudhon, another genius of social and economic thought, was the first to consider himself an anarchist, before Karl Marx, the founder of the concept known as scientific socialism. According to Proudhon, who is the author of the well-known phrase "property is theft" and who highlighted "the added value" of communal work, Saint Simon, by giving priority to producers, opened the path to social liberalism. Many questions raised today had already been asked by Saint Simon: the definition of social systems, the dynamics of industrial society, the difference between social classes, class conflicts, the importance of science and technology, changes in intellectual systems and their shared values, different modes of political domination as well as control of decision-making in industrialised societies. The list is of course inexhaustive. As I mentioned earlier, Saint Simon considered all concepts of action as an individual or collective act, but, above all, as a targeted and deliberate act. In other words, intention and social awareness play a crucial role in action, because they are based on individual interest and the interest of classes.

These concepts have been perpetuated in the works of Karl Marx. According to him, the action of "work" creates historical changes. This is why he makes an appeal, in his writing, to the proletariat to take political action to achieve the desired social changes. He considered that each political act by the proletarian class is the foundation of social revolution and the engine of major changes. For this reason, the question of action is not hidden in the various political, economic and historical analyses of Karl Marx. In his book "Capital", his analysis relies less on social action than on the study of economic structures, their conflicts and their evolution. The purpose of his analysis is effectively to discover the difference in social relations of production, the division of classes, as well as changes in production rules. According to Marx, social action is at the centre of causal relationships in the structural conflicts of conscious capitalism and is based on the mode of production. Such action is therefore conscious, but also determined by the mode of production. In other words, the actors are not free to act; they can not escape the "act".

Emile Durkheim saw Saint Simon as the first thinker having a global vision of human society. He saw it as a global entity with its own rules, its own laws. In his book "The Rules of the Sociological Method", Durkheim states that the aim of sociology is not to study economic structures, but to target, in an objective manner, "social facts", that is to say ideas, thoughts, feelings and behaviour. Social actions create behavioral patterns that exist apart from the individual, whilst having the ability to impose on him. Thus, the object of sociology is to study social actions and collective behavior in order to analyse the different models that can be imposed on a human being, much like beliefs or languages that are imposed on the people of a given region.

B - Reactionism

This type of approach to social action supposes that the meaning and understanding of action induce a procedure that can not be discerned in advance, because neither its beginning nor its end are known and predictable *a priori*; in other words, action is not determined by factors outside its will. According to "reactionism" a large part of the process of the understanding of social action is based on the interaction of actors, which can be analysed with basic common sense. The theories of Max Weber, Raymond Aaron, Alfred Schutz, Alain Touraine make-up part of this stream.

Max Weber regarded sociology as a science that attempts to understand social action whilst analysing the way in which the progress of actions and the results thereof, provide an adequate explanation of social facts. Thus in Max Weber's assessment, human behavior as social action, has objectives related to meaning that actors give to their behaviour. For him, subjectivism (the meaning which someone gives to the behaviour of someone else) is bound to objectivism (the prediction of the type of motivation that should guide the behaviour of someone in certain circumstances). The strength of Weber's theory lies in the "probabilistic" explanation of human behaviour. Weber evokes a typology of social activities in which he offers a range of different mental activities to show us, at what point, rationality alone can not have a role in social behaviour. In this typology, there are four distinct types of social behaviour:

- Instrumental action with a purpose fixed on a goal that the individual tries to achieve in a rational manner;
- Value-rational action, which could be a religious or moral value and is an action that is driven by religious and/or moral conviction;
- Affectional action which is determined by feeling and emotion;
- Traditional action that focuses on customs and habits.

It should be noted that social action can simultaneously and to varying degrees contain different forms of action. In fact, for Max Weber, the characteristics of action are the following:

- In action, the actor is genuinely active; that is to say that the individual is not an actor without a will in an economic structure, as in the thinking of Durkheim, Karl Marx or the other Determinists;

- Action has an objective (a goal, sentiment, tradition, etc...) and at the same time a meaning for others. One of the objectives of sociology is to reconstruct the meaning, expectations and attitudes of the individual. Using these three dimensions, one can explain the action of an individual.

- The third level of action is defined in the context of a social action which is related to other behaviours. We can use the term "action", when there is an act towards someone else. The act takes on a meaning. And it is during the act that one finds his orientation.

Raymond Aaron attempted to develop and utilise Weberian theory in the context of the philosophy of history, and for the purpose of opposing Marxism. According to him, the theory of action, its interpretation and understanding are at the centre of Weber's theory and abolish all the illusions of the philosophy of history, from the perspective of determinism. Human action can not be reduced to the laws and rules of nature, and it can not be predicted and studied in the same way as a physical experiment in a laboratory. A social class can therefore not adapt itself to a relatively objective reality, in such a way that one can predict the behaviour of the members of this class. It is for this reason that the historical and economic determinism in Marxist theory loses its value. To understand and interpret social events can not be an objective phenomenon.

Alfred Schutz, using the Weberian perspective, wished to understand the action of an individual through his daily action. He didn't want, as Durkheim did, to explain social facts as an objective phenomenon. For Alfred Schutz, between the behavioral objectivism of the individual (which is summarised in the form of the behaviour), and the apparent behaviour or subjectivism (which makes the individual aware of his state), there is a third method: the social world with all its institutions, is a significant world for the observer. The work of the sociologist is therefore to write about this world and explain his experiences or the experiences of others, through the world of signifier. In summary, Alfred Schutz deals with the actions of an individual in his social environment and seeks thereby to understand the inter-subjective relations of these individuals, by testing the mutual relationships of these actors. For Schutz, understanding the actions of individuals happens through the recognition of their intentions and motivations. One can prove that all social relations, understood and experienced by an individual, are centered on his world. The prototype of the relationship with the other comes about through the act of participating in the same activity in the same time-space. When examining a social activity, Schutz looks to the philosophy of phenomenology. Thus, the sociology of everyday life allows us to study through a "typification" how actors behave, whilst including the social world that surrounds them. It is in this sense that each individual has for himself "ideal types" in the Weberian sense of the term. If we understand these ideal types, we can arrive at an inter-subjective description and explore how individuals interpret their social environment in order to acquire the best behaviour towards another. A social typification is used. Using these behavioral models, the actors expect specific answers. That is why they organise their experiences in relation to their expectations in society.

Unlike A. Schutz and based on fieldwork research, Talcott Parsons establishes a model of structural functionalism. While using the ideas and theories of Durkheim and Weber, he attempts to create a general theory of action. According to this perspective, there is no fundamental difference between Durkheimian objectivism and Weberian subjectivism. According to Parsons, Human action is a set of objective and subjective behaviours, which is found in one of the following contexts:

- The biological context, that is to say the organism and all its needs;
- The psychic context, that is to say, people's personalities;
- The social context, meaning the context of sociological interaction between individuals, between groups;
- The cultural context, that is to say, norms, patterns, values, ideologies and ultimately, knowledge.

The action of man takes place in these four contexts. These contexts influence each other in an interactive way: they act and react to the forces and factors coming from each of them. The action of the actor has a purpose; the situation consists of conditions and means and ultimately norms and values in relation to which the goal has been selected. Thus, the social system is the way to organise these actions and actors. The social system must solve two fundamental questions, namely: integration and production. To do this, the social system must meet four functions: adaptation through the economy, the pursuit of goals through politics, integration through law and normative stability through socialisation. Symbolic interactionism and ethno-methodology with the work of Erving Garfinkel or the work of John Elster also falls under this perspective. In interactionism, the emphasis is on the influences that these interactions have on individuals.

John Elster, in turn, drawing on Weber's theory on rational action oriented towards a goal, studied individual actions as a primary focus. Michel Crozier, distinguishing between two systems of organisation, the bureaucratic and that of open organisation, concludes that in order to understand social actions, we must first understand the system of action. In a rigid and controlled system, such as the bureaucratic organisation system, face-to-face relationships and interactions are not permitted among members whilst in the open organisation system, this kind of relationship is not only permitted, it is much appreciated.

Alain Touraine makes a distinction between what is objective, that is to say, the structure, and what is subjective, meaning the action. According to him, the action carries meaning and sense; this is the reason why one should opt for sociology of actors rather than for sociology of society. Thus the object of sociology is no longer to study structures and social facts but social movements. It is with these movements that society continues to create and recreate itself and is transformed by conflict, negotiation and compromise.

Pierre Bourdieu, in order to understand social action, proposes that we study *habitus* to show how individual behaviour and the choices of members of society take place in the social space, to which extent models of behaviour and judgment are internalised through education. The individual tries to reproduce the behaviour models that he has learned about. The object of sociology is therefore to understand behaviour, the social agents and their practical reasoning in order to determine the *habitus* or social space.

****

In the preceding pages, we made an overview of the different sociological theories. We have seen that despite their differences, there is convergence around the fact that the social action of an individual is a conscious and intentional action. Intentional action is based on a set of data and information that the individual has. This information can derive from social structures or from interpreting the meaning of the action of others. The important thing is the way in which it is gathered, creating paradigms in which the actions of individuals in a given society are modeled. From this we can retain that "all human action is based on knowledge." In other words, the only certainty we have is that "man is never acting in complete ignorance," even the most superstitious of actions are based on a form of knowledge. This knowledge may be inexact or incomplete, false, erroneous, imposed, misinterpreted, arrogant, or based on a misunderstanding, it may be prompted by compassion, pride or any other reason, but "what is certain is that all forms of action can not be detached from any knowledge."

This point being clarified, let's look at how this knowledge has been acquired, and for this, we must return to a fundamental discourse of philosophy which is "knowledge." It is a fundamental discourse because the development of philosophy was in response to sophistry, which denied and still denies, the presence of "knowledge" in humans. However knowledge is the foundation of every ideology. Indeed, the base and foundation of every ideology is knowledge. Knowledge is the worldview of an ideology and it is in this vision that the vision of society, of man, and of history as we have learned from Ali Shari'aty, is sourced. And so knowledge constitutes the argumentative infrastructure of each ideology. By ideology I mean the harmonious system of beliefs that explains the attitudes and behaviour of individuals, which guides them to action tailored to their beliefs. Here, "harmonious" does not mean transcendental or metaphysical, although these elements fit together perfectly. Moreover, although ideology is a theoretical system, it is totally different from "theory", which is used to explain facts. Ideology is also different from religion, because ideology does not necessarily possess the sacred and metaphysical aspects that dominate religion. Ideology is in fact a theory and a belief that is used to gather all kinds of thoughts and visions of the world in a single "package" and that guides people's attitudes. It is clear that an ideology (or the "package") which has fallen into disuse, becomes adynamic, abstract and useless, can later be taken-up and transformed and made active and dynamic. Thus revived, the ideology becomes a subset. Examples: Nazism, neo-Nazism; positivism, neo-positivism...

In the construction of ideology, knowledge plays a dominant role. It is on the basis of knowledge of existence that the other elements of this system give meaning to their function and contribute to the internal interaction of the system. For some, it is not possible to define the concept of "knowledge", because this concept is so clear and obvious that it does not need to be defined. On the other hand, if we define it in a scientific manner, we risk falling into a vicious circle because if that which man knows is knowledge, then defining knowledge by using knowledge is to fall into a vicious circle and if defined otherwise, the definitions are not scientific and amount to verbiage. This is typically a sophistic argument that plays with words. We know the unknown through the known. And the known through other knowns. Also, although the notion of knowledge is clear, it should be given a definition: it is a philosophical discourse on the different types of knowledge and the means to acquire them. Identifying things based on questioning the why, the how and the how much, such are the criteria of reality, in order to recognise right from wrong.

Today, we know that despite the obstacles, limitations, errors, the individual may nevertheless proceed with a critical sense. In other words, man has the power to acquire knowledge with some degree of certainty. On the other hand, as long as man does not determine his situation, his position relative to his cognitive attainment, it is impossible for him to make a right decision and act in his environment. The reason is simple, those who believe, like the sophists, that the world is unknowable and that man lives in his inner subjectivity, fall into absolute subjectivity and do not achieve an accurate understanding of the world that surrounds them.

Having said that, my intention is to approach the discourse of knowledge from a practical point of view. My goal is in fact to establish a comprehensive categorisation of different kinds of knowledge, which give rise to different ideologies, orienting various attitudes of individuals. This is what I mean by knowledge from a practical point of view. To do that, I will try to establish a model of thought and different attitudes related to it. In other words, my goal is to make a model of different ways of thinking and the different corresponding attitudes. I will try to show that the ideologies that have the potential to mobilise individuals are based on principles and operate in zones of action.

In everyday conversation, we use the word "modelling" to describe a reality, an image and an example that people try to reproduce in their lives. For example, Che Guevara, model forf the revolutionary youth; Abbé Pierre and Mother Theresa, models of sacrifice; Gandhi, model of peace and conciliation, etc... We observe that political leaders, saints, artists and celebrities can provide examples and models. Even in the sciences, such as sociology, in order to explain social problems, we compare society to an organism whose feet are the workers, the head the political leaders, etc...This eventually led to the organicism of Herbert Spencer. Note that modelling in sociological methodology is the artificially and abstractly manufactured representation of a social fact, a "social reality." In this sense, modelling is a sociological thinking concerning an action, a social system or social position. Here the model does not recreate or reconstitute reality. In fact, it represents reality so that we can interpret it and be inspired by it. Such modelling is used on three levels. The first kind of modelling is based on the "ideal type", proposed by Weber. Here, we proceed with criticism, in other words, an exact observation of reality and empiricism, and we mentally reconstruct an infinite set of different situations. For example, the "ideal type" of feudalism and capitalism don't purport to present the concrete forms of these social and economic systems, but rather a questionable and interpretable image thereof, in order to interpret, comment on and analyse them.

Secondly, it is possible to model an institutionalised social action such as an educational method, power relations or a sports game. One must also take into account the set of relationships that show the operation of this system with its actors, their roles, their reactions, convergent and divergent. This model is the dialectical relationship between empirical observations and productions of the mind. Thus, we can begin to review and analyse them. In this case, one can arrive at a mathematical formulation, for example by observing on the one hand, trees in nature; on the other hand, by counting them, we can mentally produce the figures. These do not exist in nature.

A third kind of modelling takes into account a meaning on a more general level and which is close to a theory, to an interpretable model. In this sense, we propose a general model encompassing a vast domain of collected data and finally describe and then explain it. The integration theory of Durkheim, who claims that the individual is the result of society and that even his personal feelings come from the society that surrounds him, is a good example. In the deterministic model, society takes precedence over the individual, and through the process of internalisation and socialisation and through its institutions such as school, family, religion etc..., it imposes its values and its norms. In this sense, the moral man is the result of the human morality of the society that integrates the individual.

Another example is the theory of the civilising process by Norbert Elias. Based on this theory, becoming civilised is an evolution of personality structures. This evolution is the result of transformations in social structures. For Norbert Elias, this evolution in western Europe occurred between the years 800 to 1900. Factors such as social change, technological progress, social inequalities on the one hand and competition between individuals and social groups, on the other hand, played an important role. These factors led western societies to a concentration of population and wealth in the central state.

The modelling that I will present comes under this third level, that is to say, an explanation at a very comprehensive level. I'm trying to arrive at a theorisation and an interpretative modelling that shows a general mapping containing a large field of data, so that I can achieve a descriptive and explanatory systematisation. I must point out that such a presentation, or "geometric mapping" helps to place the subject of particular study among other subjects and clearly shows the accuracy of the understanding of the subject, as well as the transfer of the subject: that makes its learning easier.

Model of knowledge in theory

Living beings in order to survive, in addition to biological and genetic tools, require certain information to be able to use the tools they have at their disposal. In fact, whilst the foetus is forming in the womb of the mother, and after some time, a certain type of simple awareness of self and of its environment, are possible; it receives "instructions on congenital behaviour" just like its body receives genetic instructions. This "congenital conditioning" is what we call "instinct".

Instincts help creatures newly-arrived to the world, even in the womb, to have the appropriate behaviour for their own survival. The present instincts, existing since birth, include tendencies that are genetic components of the living being. Of course instincts are independent of all experiences of the environment around the living being. Instincts are inherent responses to vital motivations of the living being. In effect, instincts deriving from a genetic behavioural programme play a vital role for the living being. Pierre-Paul Grassé tells us that instinct is the innate ability to accomplish without learning.

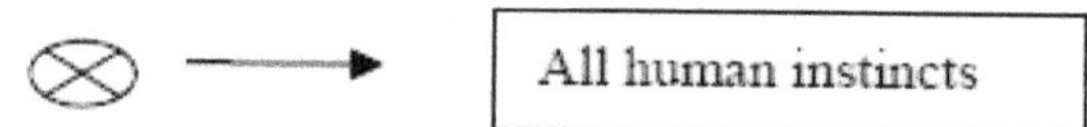

Instincts cannot be learned and long-term goals do not form a part of their operation. Instincts exist for a temporary equilibrium. For example, from an instinctive point of view, sexual relations serve to eliminate sexual appetite, and living beings during sex, do not think about the multiplication of generations or the creation of new talent or brave soldiers to serve in homeland defense. Instinct is not a function of time or a foundation of space, because it cannot adapt itself to environmental conditions, nor transform itself over the course of time. Everywhere on earth, the birds build their nests according to their instincts and spiders have been spinning their webs on the basis of instinct dating back millennia. Baby turtles run towards the sea and ducklings with their expertise and skill, cast themselves into the water and swim with ease. It should be noted that in some cases, instinctive operations require stimulants to be initiated, but once initiated, follow their natural path: the birds born and raised in a small cage, the moment when they are released from the cage, fly perfectly.

It is obviously possible for the living being to improve his instincts: the duration of singing of birds born in a cage is shorter than that of free birds, and that is due to experience helping the free birds to sing better. In other words, there is a direct relationship between instinct and intelligence. Beavers use their intelligence to improve the construction of the dams which they build.

We find therefore that certain basic principles of reason and experimentation perhaps form part of instincts. The difference between man and animal, in terms of instinctive acts, is that man's instincts, over the course of years, are gradually influenced by cultural teachings, so that after some time, the "instructions on congenital behaviour" disappear and all that remains is certain aspects of instinctive behaviour. In effect, for man, after the "Big Bang" of "birth" and after the progression of "time" and the acquisition of experience in his environment and surroundings, man acquires additional knowledge that assists him in his actions. In researching the various theories on this subject, I compared the four types of knowledge and I created a new model for the knowledge of man. These four types of knowledge are as follows:

1- Rational knowledge

This knowledge comes from the possibilities that our brain puts at our disposal, such as to analyse, to abstract, to combine, to compare, etc... This is the knowledge related to the inner life of man. This means that within the human, possibilities exist that may offer some services to him. These operations take place in the human brain, and the source of this knowledge is "reason". This "reason", over time and by soaking-up the influence of other sources that we will examine, becomes stronger, more active and more operational.

2- Experimental knowledge

This type of knowledge comes from the surrounding environment of man, namely the external existence of man, not to mention society (other people). Our experimental knowledge comes from our five senses. In experimental knowledge, we benefit from other kinds of knowledge to improve and elevate our knowledge. Observing, counting to find the frequency of phenomena, putting in order and regrouping, separating exceptions and finally deducing, concluding and generalising are the most important processes used in our experimental knowledge.

3- Intuitive knowledge

Intuitive and gnostic or mystical knowledge is an internal knowledge based on the mental state of the individual. It is the result of an intuitive meditation by man, a revelation that the individual experiences and, in some cases, he does not want to or cannot talk about it. The tool of this knowledge, according to the Gnostics, is the "heart" because the language of this knowledge is the language of the heart and not the language of the head. This means that talking about it is not possible; one can only feel it by themselves. Science today is wary of this kind of knowledge, because it does not correspond to scientific criteria, but this knowledge is very much present in people's lives, even in the scientific community. Arthur Koestler, in his book "The Sleepwalkers" talks about it brilliantly.

4- Authoritarian knowledge

This is the knowledge imposed by members of society such as the elites, intellectuals and religious, relying on beliefs and the behaviour of people and by reference to public consensus. Much of what exists in culture and tradition such as myths, maxims and popular wisdom, morality, religion, atheism form part of it. Man, without this knowledge, falls into a state of "anomie" in the Durkheimian sense of the term, and reaches a "crisis," conducts himself "unhealthily". The tool of this knowledge is "society".

The axes of knowledge

We find that these four types of knowledge can be grouped into two categories, and if we pair these four kinds of knowledge, regrouped on the basis of having the same nature, on two different axes, we obtain two spectres possessing two different natures:

1 - The axis of generalising knowledge

This is the axis of the macro world, the axis corresponding to knowledge with the power to be generalising. This knowledge is more likely to be accepted by many people. At one end of this axis there is logical knowledge; at the other end, we find experimental knowledge. These two poles are in no way opposed to each other; instead they are complementary.

2 - The axis of specification knowledge

This is the axis of the micro world and this knowledge, in comparison with the other two, is more specific. At the end of this axis we find intuitional knowledge; at the other end, authoritarian knowledge. Their common point is that they have the specificity to be less universal than the two other types of knowledge.

As we know, generalisation means to gather under a single concept singular objects in which common characteristics are recognised. This is what experimental science and reason do. "Specification" finds its meaning in relation to this definition. Specification gives distinctive features to phenomena, which are sometimes universal, so that they become personal and cultural. For example, phenomena with specific features include the arts, customs, traditions, local festivals. We can say that the axis of generalising knowledge contains the knowledge that requires less interpretation whilst the axis of specification knowledge is rather an axis where interpretation has an important place. A good example is that which Mohammad Ja'far Mossaffa offers when he says that the way of walking of someone who walks straight, bent, quickly, slowly, taking big steps or small steps: this is my observation of the way this man walks. But if I see in the manner of his walk that he is serene, superficial, modest or arrogant, from a good family or a vulgar and hooligan, etc...at this point, I have interpreted his walk. This interpretation is based on the axis of specification. In other words, a big part of what we have learned or what we teach our children is "interpretations of reality." It is obvious that we have no choice either, because if in our education, we do not use the interpretation of reality to teach our children, then we will end-up with adults who possess unrefined and scrappy thinking of reality. It is through interpretation that people can go beyond simple reality and reach imagination.

It is in the axis of specification that individual and collective identity is created. Social values appear. These values make the difference between the members of the micro-society in the macro-society and, on another level, the differences between macro-societies. Generalisation is based on observation (experience) and reasoning (argumentation), but specification is based on desire (intuition) and authority (consensus). In generalisation, one can discuss and reason, but in specification one must necessarily accept or feel, and it is only after acceptance that one can argue.

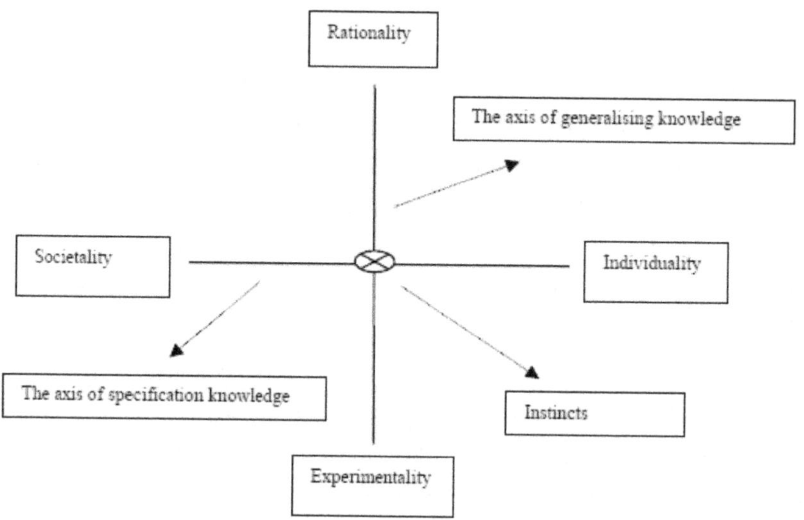

Rationality takes into account the form and appearance of reasoning: it is formal logic. Moreover, where societality is active, is where it is based on authority. When the rationality pole meets the societality pole, it generates a "formalistic" and "fundamentalist" movement. Where individuality, based on the principle of will and of emotional tendency, meets the rationality pole, this produces introversion, where interpretation is strongly present.

Introversion is a dependent variable of rationality. Experimentalism, based on external information and which does not require individual interpretation gives rise to extroversion, which is an independent variable. If experimentalism is inward-looking, then it is relativistic, because it does not have any principle *a priori*. It then forms a relativistic movement.

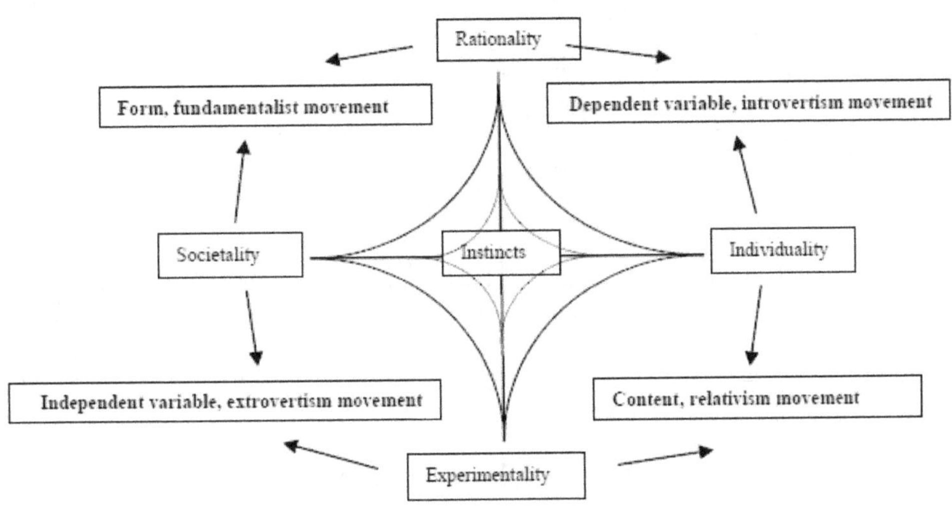

In this diagram, the further one moves away from the centre towards the sides, the more one goes away from more flexible and natural normative elements towards harder and more artificial normative elements. On the crest of each side, we find the hardest and most artificial elements. By artificial, I mean that which is contrary to the nature of man, that which was invented and created by definitions and *a priori* principles. By hard, I mean the resistance exercised by man to maintain these elements. In fact, he does everything to preserve these normative elements that establish the symbolic institution which forms and determines him.

We can therefore assign to each movement a greater or lesser degree of naturalness or artificiality. In the previous figure, the dotted lines show us this grouping. The small diamond closest to the centre is the diamond of knowledge of a more natural nature, unlike the diamond that surrounds it, farther from the centre, characterising more artificial knowledge.

Time

Instincts, over time, whilst maintaining their own existence, will be subject to change according to the four sides. Four types of knowledge develop and evolve over time. The attainments of man are the fruit of a long evolution, a historical budding, as can be seen in the following diagrams.

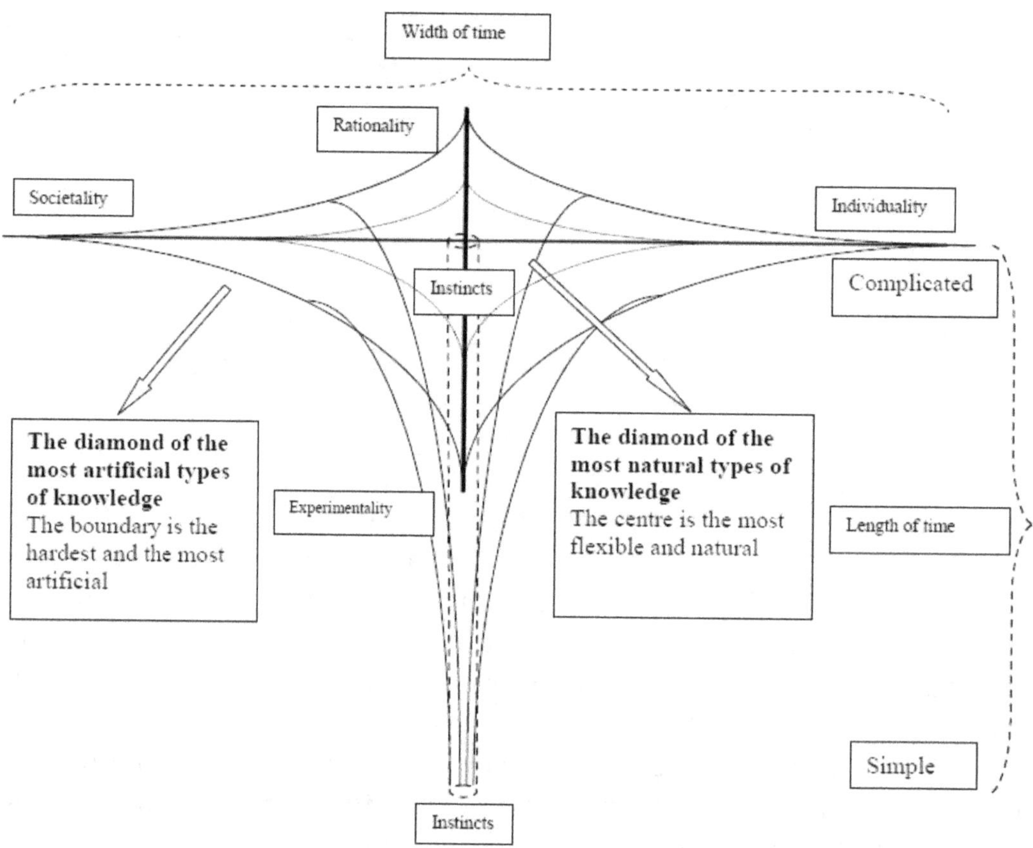

In chronological evolution, the higher you go, the more the robustness (development and complexity) and the refinement (exactitude and precision) of knowledge increase. In other words, from a more basic knowledge, we get to a more complex knowledge. From limited, universal, voluminous, opaque, ambiguous and cumbersome elements for everyday life, we reach the numerous, detailed, precise, specific, transparent, clear and less cumbersome elements for life, which are liberators. In other words, from concentration - universality in the answers to human problems - and generality, we move towards dilution - imprecision in answers to human problems - and details. The itinerary of knowledge thus begins with very few voluminous elements having between them very limited and simple relationships to get to the numerous, complex and extended elements, having very many relationships.

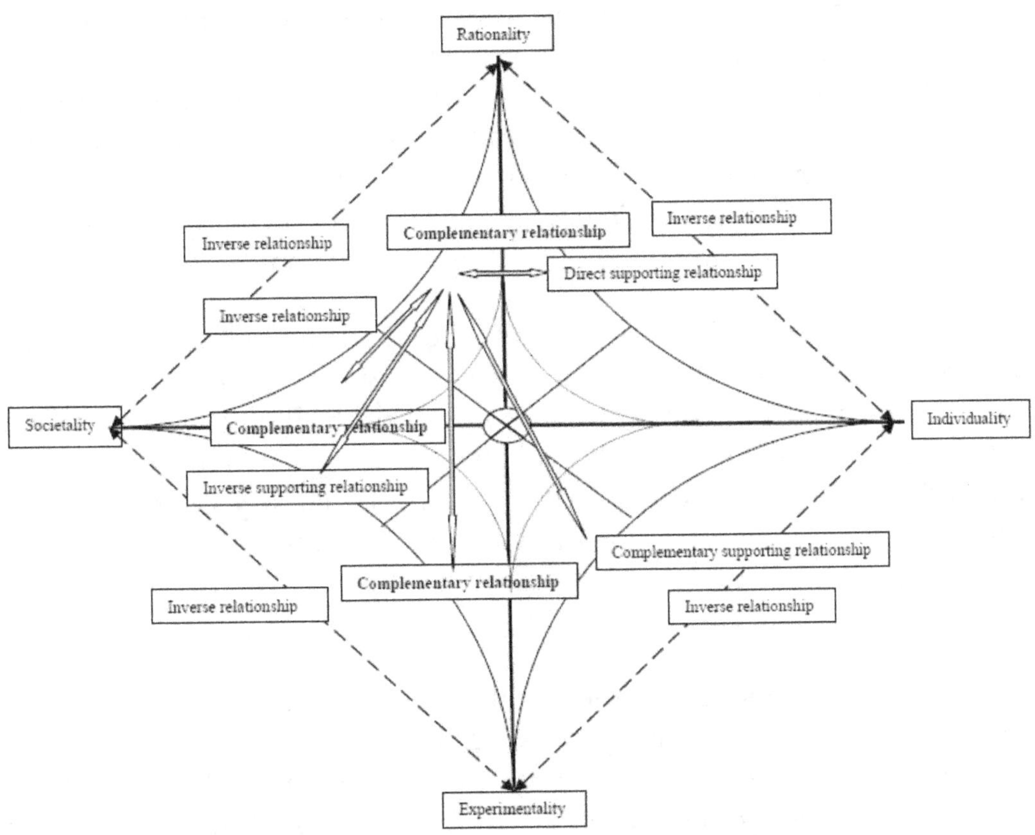

At the four apexes of the diamond of knowledge, the sources of each type of knowledge are placed. We have seen in the previous diagrams, that this diamond is divided into four zones. One can also imagine an infinite scale for each side of the diamond, the line between two apexes. Each side in turn is considered as a spectrum. Here, in order to simplify this work, I chose only the midpoint of each side, each spectrum. So I divided each side into two parts. Each zone is then divided into two parts and we thus obtain eight zones. The common point between all these zones is the central point.

These different types of knowledge, as can be seen in the above diagram, are related: either a complementary relationship or an inverse relationship. The important point that should not be forgotten is that at any given time these four kinds of knowledge are never in a contradictory relationship. They are never in conflict, because these forms of knowledge are different in nature and therefore their field of operation is different. Therefore, they cannot be in contradiction. On the other hand, if one form of knowledge is in conflict with another, one of them should be totally removed and then the individual or society falls into anomie or a lack of standards and values. Then there is a crisis which is not the normal situation for individuals and societies. The figure above illustrates these relationships…

Each apex represents one of the four kinds of knowledge and is related to the three other apexes. Each form of knowledge is on the same spectrum as the other form of knowledge that is opposite it. Each form of knowledge has an inverse relationship to the other two types of knowledge found alongside them in another spectrum. A complementary relationship means that these two forms of knowledge are part of the same, generalising or specifying, group. The complementary relationship is a fundamental and complex relationship.

The inverse relationship means that these two forms of knowledge are not part of the same, generalising or specifying, group. Their relationship is such that whenever one of the two types of knowledge takes over, the other goes below. Indeed when societality or authoritarian knowledge increases, rationality and experimentalism knowledge decrease. This does not mean that these two types of knowledge are in a contradictory relationship; they are in an inverse relationship - that is to say that both can exist at the same time, but they work in the opposite direction, relative to each other.

In the eight zones, it can be understood that each zone has a supporting relationship with a coaxial zone (which is located on the same axis) and an inverse relationship with a concurrent zone (which is located on the same side of the diamond). Each zone has a complementary relationship with the opposite zone. The very important point is the natural and evident continuity of one zone to another complementary zone. Two zones that have the same side are inverse with a different orientation, and their goals are not the same. Two zones that are found on the same axis (co-axis) are facing the same direction and have the same goals, which is why they are complementary to each other. On the basis of what we have just seen, rationality and experimentalism are complementary; individuality and societality are complementary to one another. Rationality has an inverse relationship with individuality and experimentalism, but it is quite possible that it combines with those two zones. In this sense, we have a combination of rational reasoning based on societal beliefs. For example, any fundamentalist movement comes from a combination of rational arguments and social consensus. We have seen that rationality is inversely related to consensus, so in a case like this, what we get from the relationship between reason and societality is neither rational nor societal, but this combination benefits at the same time from rational reasoning and social authority. In the fundamentalist field, when reason takes over, authority diminishes. An example is needed: in the rational fundamentalism zone, ie where rational reasoning is based on authority, dogmatism is the best example. Here, reason founds the basis of reasoning and ends with dogmas which become examples of the behaviour and beliefs of people. These rational principles will be sustained through collective support. But in the neighboring zone, that is to say the zone of authoritarian fundamentalism, where these reasonings are authoritarian in nature, based on reason, populist discourse is created. These discourses are based on the customs of society. What one should know is that the perfect model of knowledge shows us that only the thoughts which keep their relationship balanced and in harmony with other forms of knowledge, can be the most complete form of knowledge. It is necessary to know that there are four types of founding argumentations that lead to knowledge:

1- Mono-factorial knowledge

This is the most abstract argument. It is based on itself and becomes untenable. At each apex of the diamond of knowledge, there is mono-factorial knowledge: at the height of rationality, there is formal logic; at the height of societality there is absolute socialism; at the height of experimentalism there is deductionism; at the height of individuality, there is anarchism. It is obvious that a tendency like "formal logic, absolute socialism, anarchism and deductionism" not only doesn't exist in reality, but can not even exist. These diverse tendencies exist only as conceptual and complementary constructions.

2- Bi-factorial knowledge

This knowledge advances its arguments by using two factors:

A-Two factors from a complementary relationship: in this case knowledge is either in the generalising domain or in the specification domain. In both cases, the discourse is incomplete;

B-Two factors from an inverse relationship: in this case knowledge is either in the extrovertism-introvertism domain or in the fundamentalism-relativism domain.

3- Knowledge based on the reasoning common to the four movements

This knowledge stems from the combination of two zones, and there are four possibilities:

A Fundamentalism, resulting from the combination of reason and authority;
B Introvertism, a combination of reason and intuition;

C Relativism, where intuition and experience meet;
D Extrovertism, using experience and authority

4- Quarto-factorial knowledge

This knowledge is the most complete knowledge, because it uses each of the four factors to build its ideas. This knowledge, in practice, is very difficult or even improbable to achieve.

We have seen the theoretical basis of the model or diamond of knowledge. In the next chapter, we will see its application and use by social actors in their action.

The model of knowledge in practice

We have seen that human action is based on knowledge. We also saw that man does not perform an action in ignorance. If we accept these two affirmations, whilst turning towards the diamond of knowledge, we will see that humans, by creating different ideologies in different zones of knowledge, try to prepare themselves to move from thought to action. Ideology helps man so that he can give an internal coherence and logic to his own attitudes.

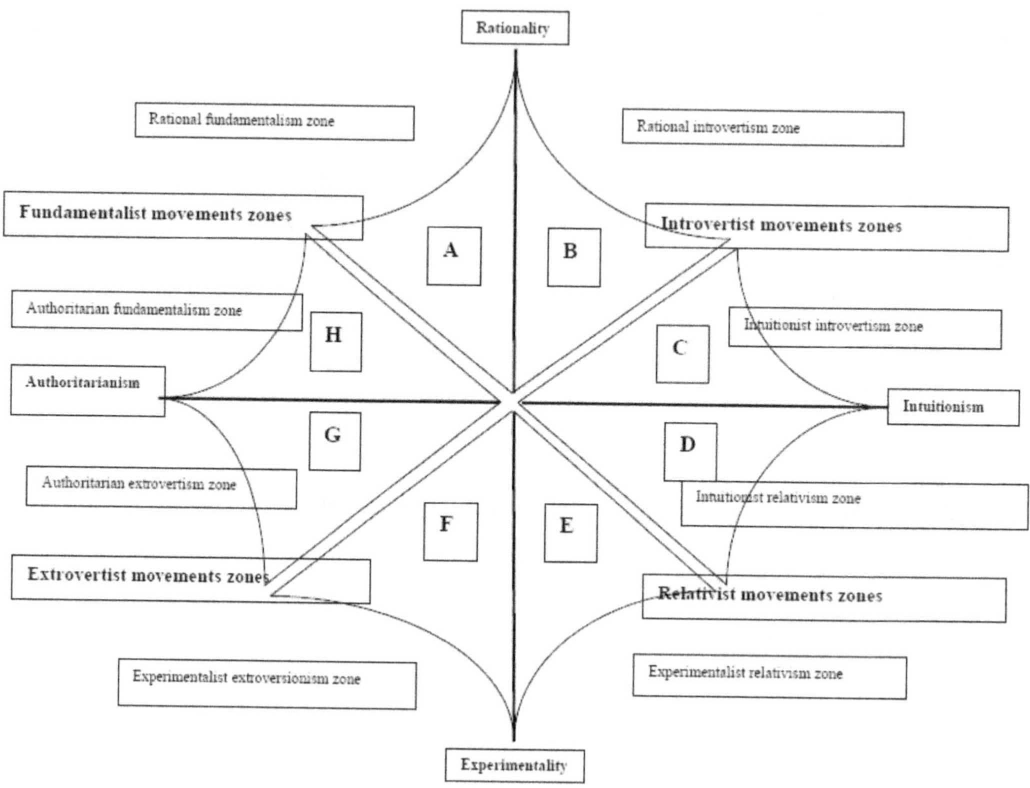

As we have seen, the diamond of knowledge is divided into eight zones of knowledge. Although these eight zones can be divided into sixteen zones, as I will explain later, we focus for the moment on the eight zones of knowledge. It should be known that individuals advance towards the method of reasoning to make their knowledge more concrete, and thereby act more easily. In other words, reasoning is the starting point of action and the manner of reasoning is the process of knowledge and ideology which we use. The way of reasoning is the theoretical starting point of action: it is the image in us of what we want to do before realising it. And so the movements of knowledge, on the basis of reasoning, consist of four broad categories: the category of the fundamentalist movement vis- à-vis the relativism movement and the category of the introvertism movement vis-à-vis the extrovertism movement.

The zone of introvertist movements (zones B and C) are areas where the source of reasoning comes from within man, that is to say, reason and intuition. In these zones, the intentions, tendencies, hopes, etc. ... of man, whether they are based on a logic or not, are motors for action. It is assumed here that neither intuition nor logic were influenced by the exterior. In practice, this is obviously not the case.

Opposite to these zones are extrovertism movements zones (zones G and F), formed from society and experience, factors external to the individual, which are not available to the individual and which he does not directly control. In practice and in the long run, however, man can influence them.

On the other side, one can find fundamentalist movements zones (zones A and H). These zones are based on exact, inflexible and indisputable principles coming from reason and society. Opposite to these zones are those of relativism movements (zones D and E) which are based on fickle intuitions and experiences through trial and error. In these movements, there are not many unchangeable principles. One must approach everything with his intuitions and examine things experimentally. In fact in order to arrive at unchangeable principles, it takes a lot of time and a lot of tests and inspections in various fields, and sometimes it is not possible to succeed. That is why, in these zones, principles are exposed in a conditional and conventional manner.

Considering these movements, we will see the macro-zones of knowledge based on the method of reasoning. This method of reasoning is actually the ideological basis for social action. We distinguish four macro-zones where, in each of these zones, a fundamental knowledge is the basis of the reasoning of this macro-zone. Other forms of knowledge turn towards this fundamental knowledge.

A. Rationality macro-zone
B. Individuality macro-zone
C. Experimentality macro-zone
D. Societality macro-zone

At the apex of each of these four macro-zones, is an ideology with mono-factorial reasoning. As I have already said, every kind of knowledge is related to other kinds of knowledge. Absolute knowledge is therefore only found in the mono-factorial definitions and reasoning; that however does not exist in practical life, and it cannot exist.

That being said, we have four types of mono-factorial reasoning, twelve types of bi-factorial reasoning, four types of common arguments. These twenty types of reasoning lead to twenty representative types of human thinking; these are actually ideologies that guide human actions. It is obvious that what I present here as representatives of human thinking are blatant examples of each type of reasoning that seemed significant to me. The reader may possibly find examples better suited to the definitions of each zone.

To find the place of an ideology in the diamond of knowledge, we must find the the genre of this ideology (fundamentalist, relativistic, introvertist or finally an extrovertist movement). We must then find towards which axis it tilts to find its macro-zone and determine its micro-zone. In defining its inclinations, we can define its place in the micro-zone. Marxism, for example, is located in the fundamentalism movement because Marxism contains principles and dogmas such as historical dialectic or dialectical materialism that claim to take political power (the state) in a society. Moreover, Marxism was able to take power and institutionalise its dogmas in some societies. It was able, in other words, to put the state at the service of its ideology. Given that Marxism is more inclined towards rational reasoning than towards societal reasoning, it is placed in zone A, in other words, it is dogmatic. And as Marxism recognises human nature, finding it to be very normal and not denying it, Marxism is placed more towards the centre of the diamond rather than the extreme tip. On the other hand, since it is based on the scientific knowledge of its time and it claims to be a result of empirical science, it is therefore closer to the axis of rationality-experimentalism and away from sophistry. In the following diagram we can see its place:

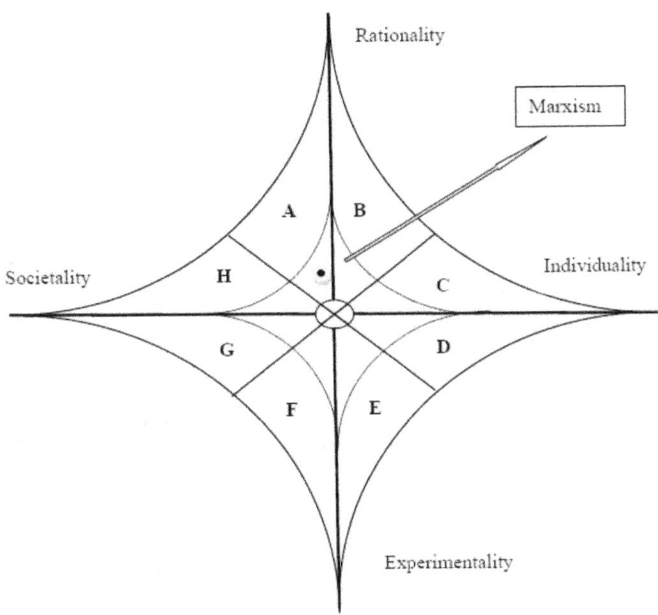

The route of Marxism is as follows: from zone A, it goes towards the F zone which is its complementary zone, and relying on the support of zone B which is its co-axis zone against its inverse supporting zone G. The E zone is the supporting zone for zone F. Its ideologies, like the ideologies of zone F and B, come to the aid of zone A. This means that the ideology and discourse of Marxists, which forms part of the discourse and ideologies of zone A, benefit from the support of the discourse in zones B and F. These zones will be clarified more in the coming pages.

A - Mono-factorial arguments

These are arguments which derive from a single factor. Such reasoning is incomplete in practice, but is useful for theoretical work and for theorising. There are four types of mono-factorial reasoning.

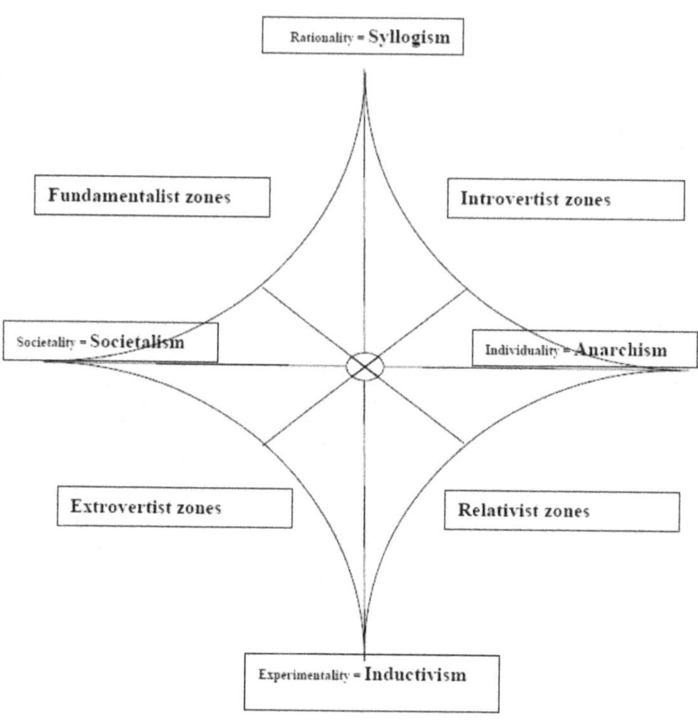

A1 - At the apex of rationality (zones A and B): syllogism

Reason and logical methods and rationales make-up, along with the other three sources, intuition, experience and society, a macro-zone which we will call the macro- zone of rationality. By rationality I mean that which is strictly logical. That which reason should respect in order not to fall into error. Syllogism is not the only purely logical and rational functioning, there is also abstraction, comparison and deduction, conjunction and disjunction (conjunctive and disjunctive syllogism) etc. Syllogism is reasoning which starts with the major (containing the attribute), then the minor (containing the subject) and finally reaches the conclusion or consequence. This is the inverse of induction which examines specifics, effects, consequences to the cause, in principle and in general. Syllogism does not offer us new knowledge, which is why this is a uniquely analytical operation, whilst induction does lead to new knowledge.

Logicism transforms all mathematical theories into logical discourse. It is reductionism in general and logical positivism in particular. For example, organicism is a kind of reductionism and not accepting metaphysical discourse in a sociological analysis is a kind of logical positivism.

A2 - At the apex of individuality (zones C and D): anarchism

Zones C and D are the zones of individuality which are crowned by anarchism. Anarchism is the group of theories and practices that are anti-power, anti-state and anti-social order of any kind. This ideology doesn't accept any limitation to the individual, either through the State or through social institutions. Its aim is to achieve a society without classes, distinctions and dominations so that people can freely participate in self-management of their society. Thus anarchism is in opposition to totalitarianism, communism, as well as capitalism and imperialism. It is also contrary to centralism. Anarchism is consistent with the socialist system: it does not want to gain political power. In anarchism, all states of the world are seen to demolish human dignity and prevent its development. Syndicalism is a legacy of anarchist thought of the 18th and 19th centuries, believing that the military and political leaders could be physically eliminated. Even today, there are anarchist terrorist organisations.

A3 - At the apex of experimentality (zones E and F): inductivism

In contrast to rationality, and on the axis, we find the zone experimentality. Inductivism is primarily a philosophical reflection, established by David Hume. According to him, the science needed to know one's object of study must use the inductive method, based on empirical observation. Such an idea has also given rise to other sciences such as statistics, probability and sampling. All these branches of science are based on the frequency of their findings. It is obvious that the accuracy of conclusions depends on the precision of data collection. If the data is not correct, the findings will not be either. As in syllogism, if the major and minor are not correct, the conclusion will not be either. For some thinkers, such as Karl Popper, despite observations from the census, we still can not scientifically generalise our conclusion because we do not observe the future to predict that future observations will confirm the conclusion of today.

A4 - At the apex of societality (zones G and H): societalism

Societality is the opposite of individuality and societalism can be one of the good ideological representatives of this zone. Societalism means total and absolute acceptance of all that comes from society such as traditions, customs, norms, institutions, in a word, the spiritual and material culture of the society. Of course one can consider a little change, due to the necessity of time, but not much. Here, collective reason and collective objectivity are supported by collective authority.

Although seemingly the existence of such a trend among people seems very strange and improbable, one must know that no society can exist without societalism. Symbols are to be found in this zone. Man and humanity can not survive without symbols. One of the most common symbols for social life is language. Culture is a set of symbols.

B - Bi-factorial Reasoning

Bi-factorial reasoning is the most common type of reasoning and there are twelve versions. Based on two factors, these arguments translate perfectly in practice and are scattered throughout human history.

B1 - Rationality zone (zones A and B) Reason - Authority side: Dogmatism

In the zone of rational fundamentalism, where rational reasoning creates authority, that is to say where reason forms thought and where social authority sustains it, dogmatism is its best representative. In this case, authority is rational. Dogmatism believes in a true and certain knowledge, and that is why it is not in agreement with either skepticism or with opportunism. It is also contrary to sophistry. In other words, dogmatism expresses its thoughts with the support it has from authority and without leaving the least chance of incorrect arguments. Kant used this term against criticism. For Kant, dogmatism does not support metaphysical relativism. For Auguste Comte, dogmatism belongs to the theological period; once it reaches the positivist period, it is eliminated. In politics, the dogmatists are politicians who, without taking political, economic or social changes into account, refer all the time to the principles of their political party. In the history of the communist party, after the revisionism movement, the communist dogmatists, considering these movements as a right-wing deviationism, sided with doctrinalism or a left-wing deviationism. In dogmatism, elites, experts, supervisors etc are very important and the officials of society are doing everything possible to gain their support. The people and the man on the street have nothing else to do but follow the dogmas and their definitions.

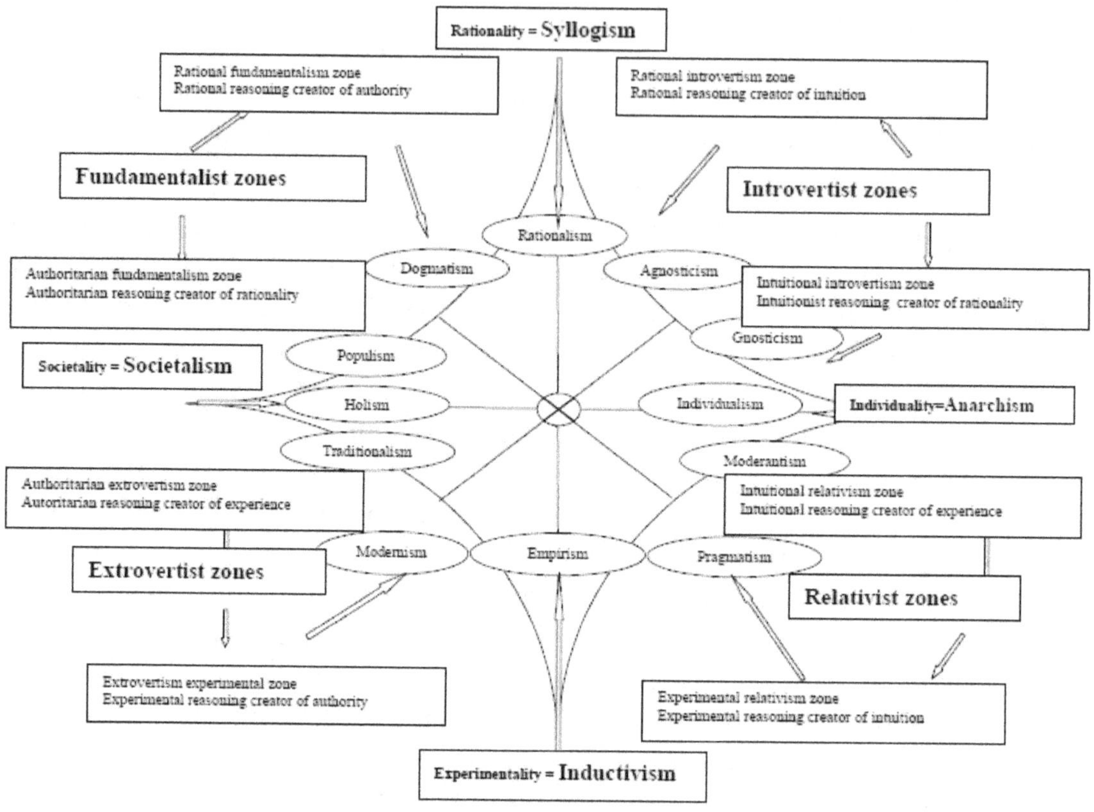

B2 - Rationality zone (zones A and B) Reason - Experience side: Rationalism

Here, rational reasoning creates experience. This means that, firstly, reason traces what experience should do, then, in going towards experience, trying to reproduce in the best way, the principles it had established at the beginning. Theorising in science is an example. Mathematics is a very good example. The principles of mathematics do not exist in nature; they are merely theorems to advance rational reasoning.

Experience serves reason; simple data should be treated with reason so that it makes sense and has meaning. It is reason that reconstructs anew observations and draws useful meanings from them. In other words, it is reason that gives them meaning.

Rationalism recognises intuitive, traditional or even theological knowledge as well as divine revelations, provided we can find a causal and intelligible explanation which accords with reason.

Rationalism is opposed to utilitarianism and hedonism. Rationalism is a valuation tool whilst logicism is only a tool to distinguish the truth from falsity.

B3 - Rationality zone (zones A and B) Reason - Intuition side: Agnosticism

Agnosticism relates to an ideology that does not cover areas beyond experience and observations. It is a perspective with rational arguments about the disqualification of man. He tries to understand and know some subjects such as metaphysics and theology, the existence or nonexistence of God. There is no dogma in this thinking; it differs from antitheism, atheism, deism, skepticism and apathy. There are agnostics who say we should wait for scientific progress to find answers for certain questions; there are others who say that we will be unable to answer certain questions because they are beyond the means of understanding.

B4 - Individuality zone (zones C and D) Intuition - Reason side: Gnosticism

Here reasoning is intuitive and benefits from the help of rationality. Gnosticism seems to me to be a good example for this ideology group. Gnosticism is a category of schools of philosophy and theology that have existed since the first century or even earlier, in Mesopotamia, Egypt, Palestine and Syria. The common point of all these schools of thought is the pretence of certain inner knowledge or metaphysics called Gnosticism. Many of these schools are of Christian tradition, but there are also Jewish, Manichean and Muslim Gnostics. We can refer to four features in particular of Gnosticism:

A - Dualism in creation. According to Gnostics, this world is in effect a world of evil, disease, injustice, tyranny and of need; such a world can not have been created by a good god. There must therefore exist a good and a bad god: god of light and a god of darkness. Man is the result of the combination of light and darkness. Man, having forgotten that his origins are also linked to a good deity, wanders and is lost in this world. But he can, whilst turning towards his knowledge, through meditation and inspiration, find his origins. The Gnostic says "be in this world without being of this world";

B - The idea of having to save man comes from the fact that the principle is duality. As man is trapped in this world, the subject of man's end is raised and we ask if he will one day be saved. Salvation for the Gnostics is a metaphysical and spiritual salvation, and it is by offering prayers that we can get there. For some Gnostic sects, leaving the world and retreating is another possibility;

C - Skepticism also stems from the fact that this world is the kingdom of evil. It is therefore necessary to avoid and beware of it. It is necessary for some Gnostics, to be deprived of the good carnal things in life, like getting married, eating meat, etc...;

D - The Creator is the father, the absolute light and the origin of existence of life. The characteristics of this father are not very clear, but we know that his creatures are almost perfect, and if these creatures are made in his image, then he is everywhere in this present world; this is where the idea of pantheism comes from. In pantheism, everything in this world represents the Creator.

Gnosticism is the opposite of agnosticism and dogmatism. It moves away from populism; by withdrawing from the mass, it moves towards sects and constitutes a kind of sectarianism, not necessarily political. Theosophy and theosophism come from Gnosticism.

B5 - Individuality zone (zones C and D) Intuition - Authority side: individualism

In individualism, the principle is to give preference to the rights, interests and individual values in relation to society. The independence of the individual vis-à-vis society, caste, family, tribe, which impose all their rules and standards on the individual, is required. The individual is therefore opposed to all the duties that these diverse structures require. In politics, individualism requires a limitation of state power, of traditionalism, of despotism and of totalitarianism. It even opposes unlimited and overly libertine liberalism. For Alexis de Tocqueville, individualism is the consequence of democracy and for Durkheim, it is the logical result of the division of labour in society. Individualism is different from egotism because its objective is not to defend the personal interests of the individual, but the interests of individuals. For example, voluntarily becoming a member of a club is not a contradiction with regard to individualism.

B6 - Individuality zone (zones C and D) Intuition - Experience side: Moderantism

After the French revolution, moderantism was the name that the left of parliament, who favoured state terrorism, gave to the right who were against this sort of practice. Moderantism in this context means mercy, tolerance, carelessness, which in politics and in culture, leads to a coexistence of citizens, putting aside all kinds of doctrines and dogmas. This coexistence should not be based on doubt in relation to these principles and beliefs; it should instead be based on respect for the freedom and rights of others. This is the result of a reflection on the history of humanity which has learned from moderates to accept the multiculturalism of the modern world and that in pursuing war we only achieve the destruction of man. This moderantism is different from the tolerance or the kindness that are preached in different religions. In moderantism, there is no notion of the complete man or the perfect man. It sees man as he is, with his strengths and weaknesses. Thus moderantism is humanistic, individualistic, relativistic and skeptical. It is in contradiction with fundamentalism because it does not believe in absolute truth. According to moderantism, the concentration and centralisation of power corrupts.

B7 - Experimentality zone (zones E and F) Experience - Intuition side: Pragmatism

Pragmatism is a philosophical movement according to which that which is functional and provokes a conclusive result is more important than other things. This notion, without denying logic, is opposed to the notion of Cartesian rationalism. Indeed, in this thinking, reflection revolves around that which is practically operational and functional, because only the functionality of a phenomenon gives meaning and significance to the phenomenon. In this sense, "thought" is merely a tool to achieve a result and is not important in itself. Here "*a priori* truths" do not exist, it is rather experience that manifests "truths." Unlike rationalism, pragmatism is consistent with utilitarianism and hedonism. In utilitarianism, the well-being of everyone is taken as the only moral criterion. According to utilitarianism, the actions to be performed by the individual are fair and create happiness for the whole society. Hedonism assumes that the purpose of life is to derive maximum pleasure, material or otherwise.

B8 - Experimentality zone (zones E and F) Experience - Reason side: Empiricism

Experimental reasoning, based on reason, tells us that the main traits of thought must derive from experimental observations. Reflecting in a rational manner therefore derives from observations. Empiricism does not give importance to *a priori* principles and is based only on sensory experiences in order to build knowledge. The method is therefore inductive, from the concrete to the abstract.

B9 - Experimentality zone (zones E and F) Experience - Authority side: Modernism

Modernism is a collection of cultural movements that have shaped Western societies since the late 19th century in various fields such as architecture, music, literature, theology and Catholicism etc... The summit of modernism in art is to be found around the second world war. Following that, there was so-called post-modernism. Modernism means benefiting from scientific and technological progress. Obviously, with this idea, there are social values involved in social developments and changes such as citizenship, democracy, universal suffrage, freedom of expression, freedom of speech, etc…

In modernity, economic aspects conflict with social aspects. For example, in modernity, short-term gain conflicts with aspects of environmental protection, such as avoiding the pollution of nature and the wasting of energy.

The objective of modernisation is to optimise economic and technological production and that living standards increase. Thus, along with modernisation, social and psychological changes also appear. In modernity, experimental reasoning creates authority, that is to say that authority is based on experience and it is for this reason that innovations and changes have the force of law. Modernity does not accord much importance to history, except where it can provide added value for innovation and change.

B10 - Societalism zone (zones G and H) Authority - Experience side: Traditionalism

Tradition is a set of norms, institutions, beliefs, values, rules, etc... which, in the name of the necessary continuity between the past, present and future, is imposed upon society. Thus traditionalism is a world vision that is based on this indisputable evidence of continuity. In traditionalism, customs are the most rational part and tradition is the most experimental part. Traditionalism is consistent with conservatism, reactionism and ethnocentrism. It does not want change. Individualism and internationalism do not have a place. Innovations are rarely accepted and when they are to be accepted, tradition tries to adapt them to its traditional norms and beliefs so that they are digestible for people. In traditional societies, time and therefore the pace of life, is very slow and does not compare with the rhythm of life in other societies. Traditionalism is opposed to modernism.

B11 - Societalism zone (zones G and H) Authority - Intuition side: Holism

Holism considers existence in its entirety and independently of its founding elements. According to holism, as soon as we can understand and grasp an element, we have the ability to study all that encompasses it. This idea first appeared from Hegel with the notion of totality and from Gestalt psychology where the human psyche is whole and can not be divided into parts. In this context we must understand this concept in the anthropological sense of Louis Dumont. For him, this reality is found in all situations in which social authority is imposed in the name of community orders and values and where individuals are diminished vis-à-vis this social authority, this policy and this sacred will. Most societies value social order. Each member adapts to the values of the society which is born whole. This is holism, but there are other societies where individuals are given priority. For these societies, each man is the crystallisation of all mankind. In this perspective, each person is equal to the others. This is individualism. Attention must be paid to the fact that in societalisation, order and social authority are imposed on society; in holism, by contrast, it is the general culture of the society which is imposed on the entire population.

B12 - Societalism zone (zones G and H) Authority - Reason side: Populism

Populism is a good example of authoritarian reasoning which creates reason, namely the kind of reasoning in favor of social authority which drains reason. The most important tool of populism is custom. It consists of all social habits or patterns of belief that people in a society have accepted and followed, based on popular reason. Custom is the rational part of tradition and it takes advantage of the credibility it creates and the moral domination that it engenders...

The most important function of custom is its application in legislation as well as in complementary law to jurisprudence and written laws. Written laws are the laws established by a judicial body, whilst customs are unwritten laws and contain contracts and practices observed by the members of a society in their social and business relations. Customs are legally allowed in many countries of the world. For example, in England, the legal system is composed of three elements, namely: equity, laws and customs.

In populism, certain groups, certain status or social classes, in different aspects such as inheritance, power, wealth, status, etc ... are more elevated than others. Populism is in agreement with them and is accompanied by relationism, theologism, a social caste system, the oligarchy, the aristocracy, etc... Elected officials and experts who have gained their status due to their superior adaptation to social norms and values, hold a very high place in the social hierarchy, but the elites and intellectuals are, in a populist society, on the margins thereof. In principle, populism does not accept intellectuals, because as in any fundamentalist thinking, it is opposed to changes. It is xenophobic and religion and homeland are its watchwords. It is also opposed to individualism, egalitarianism and liberalism.

It should be well understood that custom is both the creator of religion and a creature of religion. In a sense custom takes precedence over religion, because its metaphysical ideas emerged long before the emergence of myths and religions. Religion is a more recent thinking that makes these same metaphysical ideas consistent. But once religion is established, it influences and creates new customs. We understand from that, that from the same basic religion, we can have several other trends from this same religion, which belong to different societies with their different customs. That's why today, there are different interpretations of the same religion, because, as custom is necessarily and inevitably doomed to change, religion also changes. This explains Shia Islam, mystical Islam, Sunni Islam, revolutionary Islam, passive Islam, aggressive Islam...

C - The common reasonings of the four movements

The common reasonings are those corresponding to the middle of the two small zones. These are the inter-zonal reasonings that help to precisely delimit the borders of each zone. Such knowledge can be spread on both sides and can penetrate one of the two sides more than the other. It can not, however, be under the influence of the more remote zones. In fact, their area of action is only in the two neighbouring zones. Do not forget that in this essay, I am only concerned with the reasoning that lies in the middle of two zones, but other parallel interfaces exist, as can be seen in the following figure:

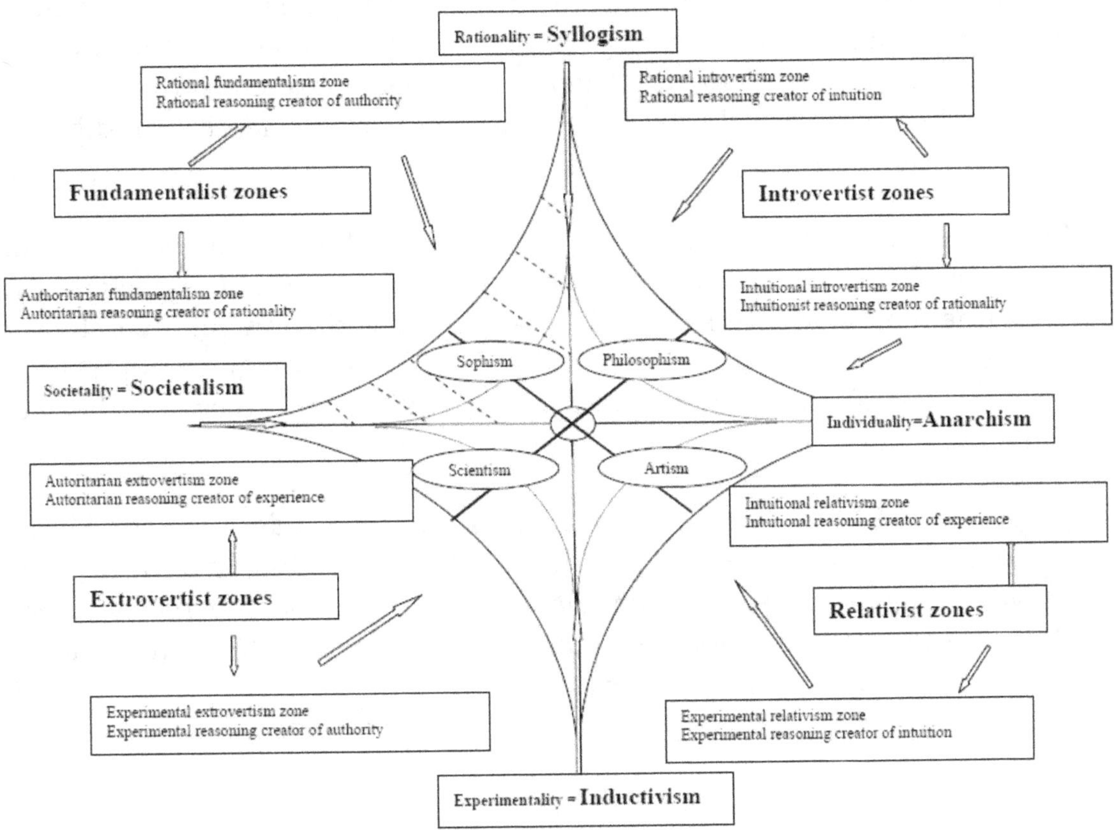

As can be seen, four kinds of ideological reasoning or arguments can be imagined: sophism, philosophism, artism and scientism. If in the field of fundamentalism, where there is sophism, we design parallel interfaces, the interfaces of sophism approaching rationalism, are charged more by rationalism, and those which approach authority are the ideological sophist reasonings charged more by authority.

C1 - The interface of the fundamentalism Reason - Authority domain: Sophism

Sophism is a kind of reasoning that is logical in appearance, but it is neither valid nor true. Unlike paralogism, the purpose of sophism is to induce another to make an error, by making false syllogisms and by using enthymemes and rhetoric, the listener is mislead. The objective in sophism is in fact to convince the listener. The logical and scientific credibility of reasoning is not its objective.

Sophism has existed for a long time; not only has it not left the human mind, but it also became institutionalised in the legal field. Indeed, lawyers conclude their instructions and their work by making an oath to defend the interests of their client by any means. Such an oath is a sophist oath, because the objective is not to uncover the reality, but to ensure the clients interests.

In politics and in business, sophist reasoning exceeds all other kinds of reasoning. The more politics becomes in effect a profession and the more it moves away from political convictions; in business, the more products there are and the more open the market is, the more sophist reasoning finds areas where it can propagate more and more.

C2 - The interface of the Introvertism Reason - Intuition domain: Philosophism

Philosophy is a set of studies, reflections and considerations with a very high degree of generalisation, which tries to find order in knowledge and human knowledge. Philosophy is an attempt to find the truth of things, to create relationships between them, understand human values and concepts and comprehend human thinking. It uses logic and reason by using science in general. Philosophy is different from science that is based on experience; it is also different from theology based on revelation and it is different from sophistry which consists of convincing the listener. The result of philosophical reflection is not experimental and has no experimental verification; it does not seek to sanctify its subjects. It doesn't try either to have its results accepted in the pursuit of a goal or to convince others. For philosophy, raising questions and trying to find answers remains a final goal. Philosophism means therefore the researching and study of different areas, and with regard to different questions of the material, moral, religious nature etc... with details, without being committed to this or that trend. Philosophism is concerned with different theorisations in order to find new approaches to understanding the world. From the methodological point of view, it is a useful approach, but in extreme cases, especially in the humanities and particularly in psychology, philosophism becomes mere useless chattering.

C3 - The interface of the Relativism Intuition - Experience domain: Artism

Artism is based on the theory of "art for art's sake" which is one of the consequences of Western modernism of the 19th century. This theory, in fact, dates back to the 18th century and is rooted in the thinking of Kant: theoretical reason in order to know things; practical reason in order to understand moral principles and the faculty of judgment in order to distinguish beauty and feel pleasure in experiencing beautiful things. Reflecting, for Kant, is a human activity that takes place in both practical reason and theoretical reason. The criteria for judging a pretty thing depends neither on theoretical reason nor on practical reason. We can not say therefore that a work of art is beautiful because, reasonably, it's beautiful. Or that it's beautiful because everyone says so. Or that it is not beautiful because our point of reference says that it isn't. Kant is therefore, in some ways, founder of the theory of "art for art's sake". In 1818, Victor Cousin in his course "Lectures on the True, the Beautiful, and the Good"" used this expression. In 1834, the critic Sainte-Beuve designated a group of young founders of the magazine Le Globe, the school of art for art's sake. In the second half of the 19th century, the Parnassian movement emerged.

During the 20th century with its school of formalism, the theory of art for art's sake appeared again. Left-wing thinkers and existentialists were quick to criticise and attack it. Art for art's sake is in fact a reaction to literary and artistic romanticism and romanticism, in turn, is a reaction to the positivism and scientism of the 17th and 18th centuries. Proponents of the school of art for art's sake wanted, whilst using artistic language, to present the emotional and sentimental side of the human species compared to the rigour of scientists. For them, art is a means of expressing the desires and dreams of the human being. Art for art's sake has therefore become a movement aiming towards the simple creation of a work of art in itself. The message of artistic work does not matter; it is the technique and skill which prevail. The manner of expression is more important than the content of the work of art. The effect that a work of art has on people is more important than its message and its contents.

Ideological movements and moralists are, of course, opposed to this vision of art, but it is important to know that artism is not necessarily immoral. It is in fact amoral. Formalism goes along the same vein as artism. According to formalism, the difference between poetry and prose is a formal one, not a difference of content. For formalists, in music, there is no content, whether it is defending a cause or not. Artism is, involuntarily, an elitist movement, because only the elites can understand the message of artists.

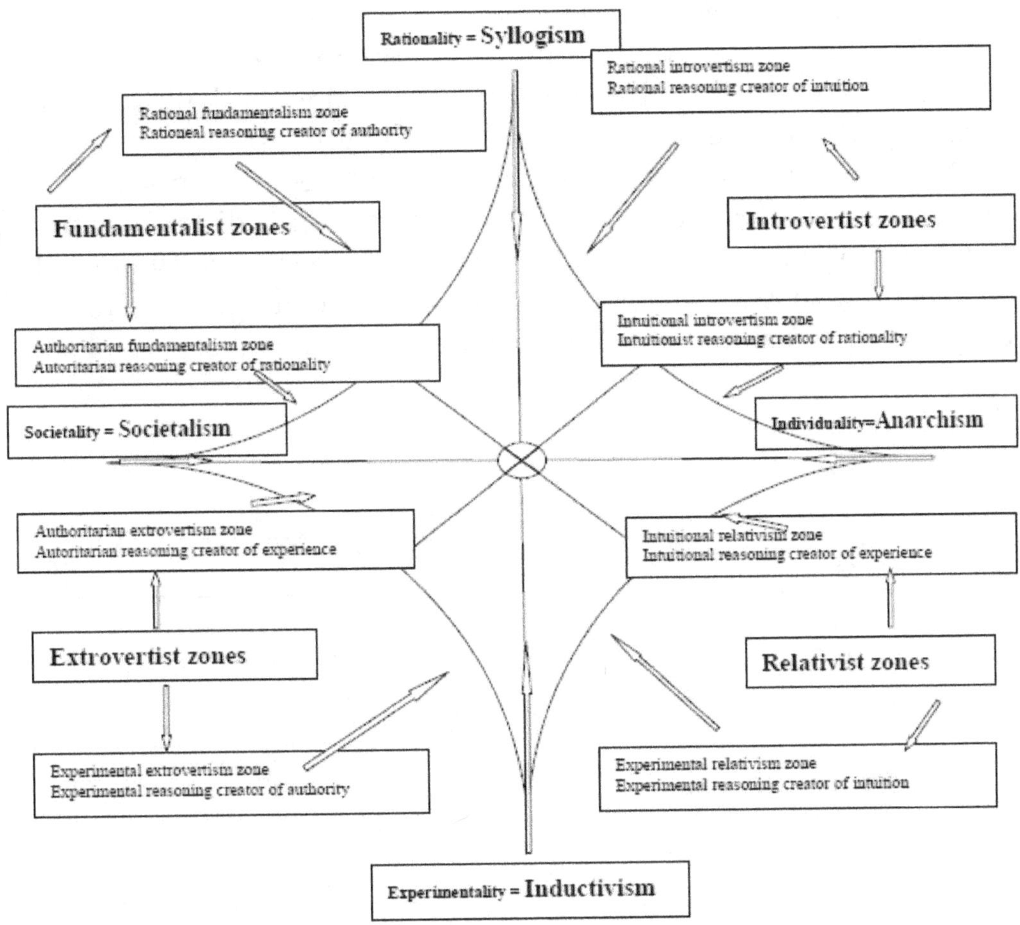

C4 - The interface of the Extrovertism Experience - Authority domain: Scientism

Scientism is a thinking according to which the only way to find valuable knowledge comes from the positive sciences; the only role of reason is therefore the role it plays in constructing science, and nothing further.

For scientism, scientific methods should use in any domains, be they material or spiritual, all the cultural, moral or philosophical domains, because only science can respond to all moral problems and save humanity from ignorance. For every problem, a universal and comprehensive response exists, that supersedes people's opinion, that is impersonal. A good education can illuminate the way for people not to fall into the darkness of metaphasic and theological delusion or hallucination. It is science which can offer a rational management of society. In fact, society should be guided by a kind of combination between the aristocracy of the experts and the technocracy of technicians and distanced from the bureaucracy of politicians. When it comes to the bureaucracy of politicians, democracy, citizenship, theology etc…have no meaning, as the members of society are not equal in the management of society.

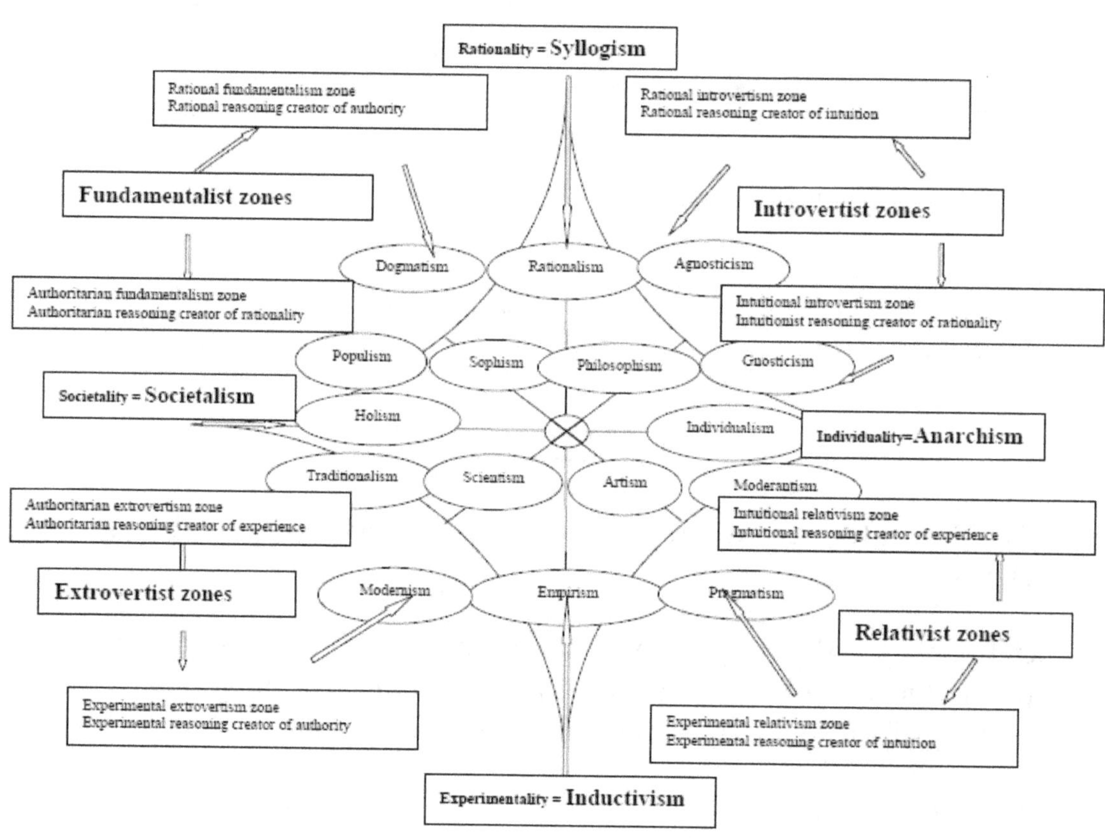

D - Quarto-factorial reasoning

These are the reasonings that are based on the four sources of knowledge in their proper place. Achieving such a feat requires a lot of mental power, which is not something everyone is capable of. It takes the whole man, as sought by Diogenes with his lantern searching in broad daylight and at whose service Hafez wanted to be because he was detached from all dependencies of this world. The whole man is one who uses his common sense, without either love or hate. But in practice, these arguments are made by actors by amalgamating ideas coming from all directions.

Diamond of knowledge and time

I will explain here the diamond of knowledge and its evolution over time. As can be seen in the following figure, in order to simplify my explanation, I am only presenting two macro-zones, namely 'individuality' and 'societality'. These two macro-zones are located on the specification axis of knowledge. As we now know, these are two complementary zones.

In this figure, H1 represents the zone of the internal part of the diamond, the most natural state: authoritarian extrovertism along with authoritarian reasoning created by rationality. Beside H1, there is H2, that is to say the same zone, but located in the external part of the diamond, that is to say the most artificial state of authoritarian reasoning created by rationality. I have indicated these two areas using the letter H, because they are the modern zones. But in reality, these zones are to be found in the oldest h1 and h2 zones. In other words, h1 and h2 are the history and antecedents to the H1 and H2 zones.

It remains to be seen what the history of each zone is and to situate them in the diamond. It should be known, as can be seen in the following figure, that the historical antecedents of a new zone may continue to exert their influence. In other words, h1 may still exist, but it is located in the central part of H1. By observing this figure, we realize that h2 has, historically, more or less disappeared, and the reason is simply its rigidity and lack of flexibility…

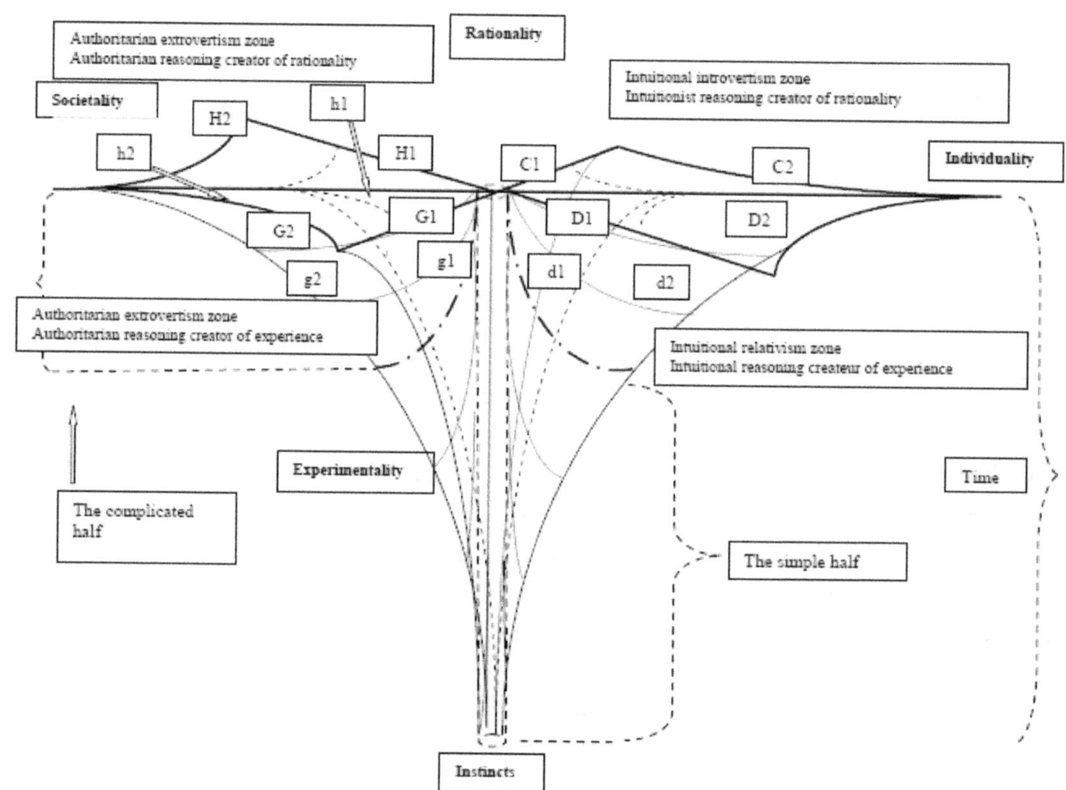

I must confess that I do not know the age of many of the elements of the different zones. It is not easy to find this out, extensive studies and investigations are required in order to properly determine the age of an element. That is why I only present one of the zones for, which it seems to me, there is sufficient information.

The intuitional introvertism zone is the zone in which intuitional reasoning creates reason, that is to say that basically intuition and reason serve the rationalisation of intuition. The most representative ideology of this zone is gnosticism and consists of a triangle, composed of gnosticism, philosophism and individualism. In the area of C1, this zone which is closer to the centre of the diamond, we will see gnostic tendencies that have closer relations with philosophism and individualism. In my view, the works of a very large number of Iranian classical authors, such as Hafez, Rumi, Saʿdī, and Khayyām, for example, are to be found at this part of the triangle. They are the ones designated by Iranians under the name of 'âref'. This part of the gnosticism zone is closer to its complementary zone, meaning the populism zone.

In the C2 region, this same gnosticism has a more rigid manner and takes the form of uncompromising and extremist sects. These insist on abandoning the world and people to move away from tyranny, despotism or earthly love in order to focus on heavenly love.

In trying to establish the age of the two regions of the gnosticism zone, we understand that among the four features that we mentioned above, pantheism is the oldest. Indeed, today's pantheism comes from the animism of yesterday and therefore the c2 region should be the place of animism which after experiencing changes and developments in the course of history and having internalised dualism, salvation and pessimism, and after passing through the period of shamanism, arrived at the c1 stage and was transformed into Hinduism, Buddhism and Jainism.

According to animism, all beings, living or non-living, have meaning, intelligence and personality. In primitive societies, stones, woods, rivers, mountains, deserts, poultry, reptiles, for example, all possess a soul and man has to satisfy them so that nothing bad happens to him. Some traces of these ideas still exist in the Japanese religion Shinto (the way of the gods).

Animism turns into shamanism, which does not have a single God. It is through incarnation that the human mind is perfected. With magic, one can dominate the forces of nature so that they serve man. This religion is still alive in the Mongol tribes, among the American Indians and Eskimos. Shamans are priests and have a relationship with supernatural forces. As in animism, shamanism also believes that man must protect himself from visible and invisible forces.

Hinduism, the world's third largest religion after Christianity and Islam, has neither a prophet nor dogma to follow, but having five thousand years of history, is one of the oldest religions in the world. It consists of a set of beliefs and polytheistic philosophical thoughts. One can gain knowledge, through the texts of the Upanishads, on a complex system of customs and mystical and Sufi beliefs. According to the Upanishads, a total soul exists that all spirits join after death, in other words, a manifestation of pantheism. Yoga is a way to accelerate this unification and the incarnation consists of being present several times in this world, of gnostic pessimism, to perfect it and deserve this unification.

Buddhism, a close relative of Hinduism, is based on four principles such as life is only suffering and dissatisfaction coming from desire and from attachments that must be eliminated to end suffering. To achieve this, we must deny ourselves and practice austerity. In this way, humans can reach nirvana or beatific annihilation. One can find this religion in Ceylon, Burma, Japan, India and China.

Jainism, which emerged as a reaction against Hinduism and Buddhism, is against the killing of animals, even dangerous animals, because they are part of the soul and total existence. For Jainists, everything is eternal in this world. Through incarnation, the human soul retains its identity and a Jainist, usually after nine incarnations, reaches nirvana.

****

We have seen the evolution of the diamond of knowledge, but there is one last point. The historic route of the evolution of the model of knowledge is not straight as we have seen so far, but a little curved. This route has a very distant past (bottom left) to the present time (top right). Such a move shows us the age of the left side of the diamond, that is to say that the macro-zone of fundamentalism bends and spills towards the modern and new side of the diamond, that is say the right side, the macro-zone of relativism.

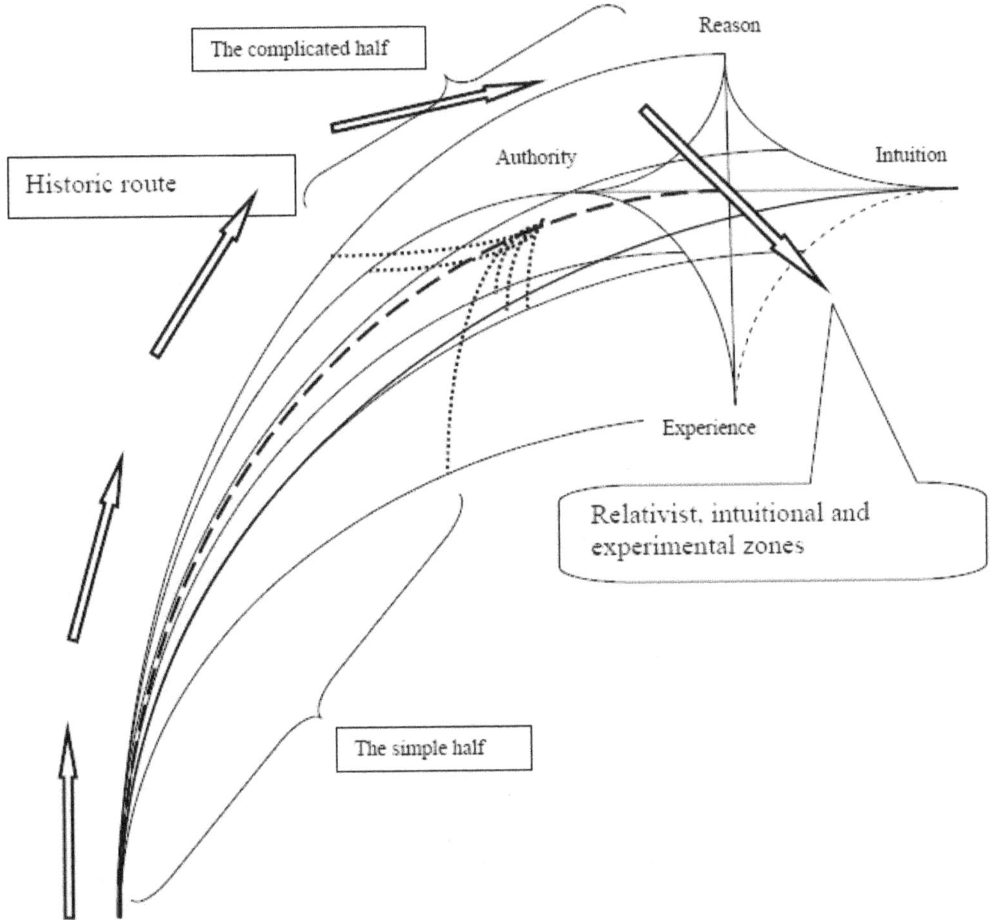

In effect relativism is a modern movement, more vast and developed than fundamentalism. Fundamentalism is more limited, harder and more closed.

This shows us that reason and consensus, which are the essential foundations of fundamentalism, give way gradually to intuition and individual experiences. The orientation of human knowledge therefore comes from the macro to the micro. In other words, the human world goes from the closing towards the opening, from principles to the concrete, from authority towards moderantism, from elitism towards populism, from simplicity towards complexity, from certainty towards doubt, from domination towards collaboration, from centralism towards plurality, and finally from praise towards rationalism.

Postscript

The diamond of knowledge, with its small internal diamonds, forms a sort of two-dimensional spectrum. It is a Cartesian coordinate system to locate the geographical position of a school of thought, an idea of a person, a community, a group or a society.

The diamond of knowledge can therefore be used in research to generate the necessary criteria for questioning and at the same time be used to illustrate the results of studies. In this case, we obtain a form that easily demonstrates the values of each individual or community or society.

For example, a large number of Iranian writers and intellectuals think that t models of thinking of Iran are quite distinct from those of Westerners: actually Iranian thinking would turn more on the societality-individuality axis and would be inclined towards societality and social authority. While, according to these thinkers, the West would be more centered around the axis of rationality-experimentality with a slope towards individuality.

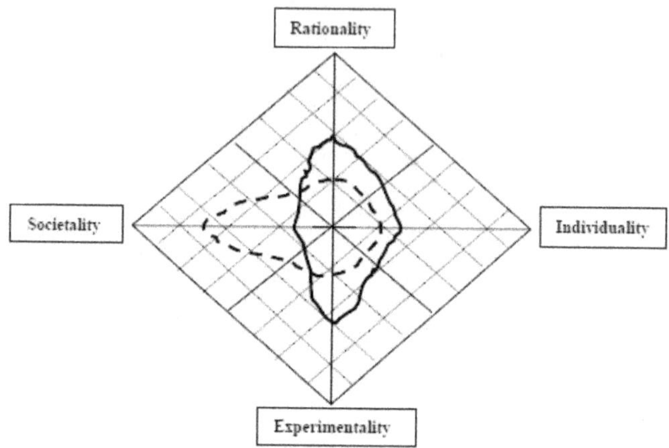

One can of course have different abstract graphics in this diamond of knowledge. For example, the chart number 1 corresponds to a entirely rational man. The second, a man of absolute authority and finally, the third, a perfectly balanced man.

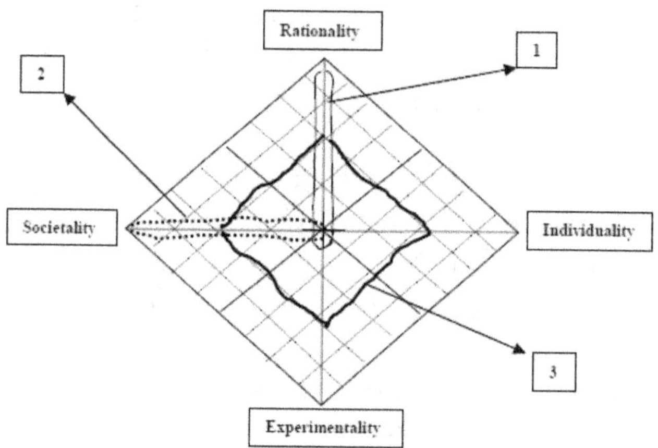

If in a survey conducted by questionnaire in which the focus is on the four sources of knowledge on the two axes, we obtain the values 55.40, 68.80, 62.60 and 66.60 out of 100 respectively for societality, individuality, rationality and experimentality, the sum of vectors will give us the result as shown in the figure below:

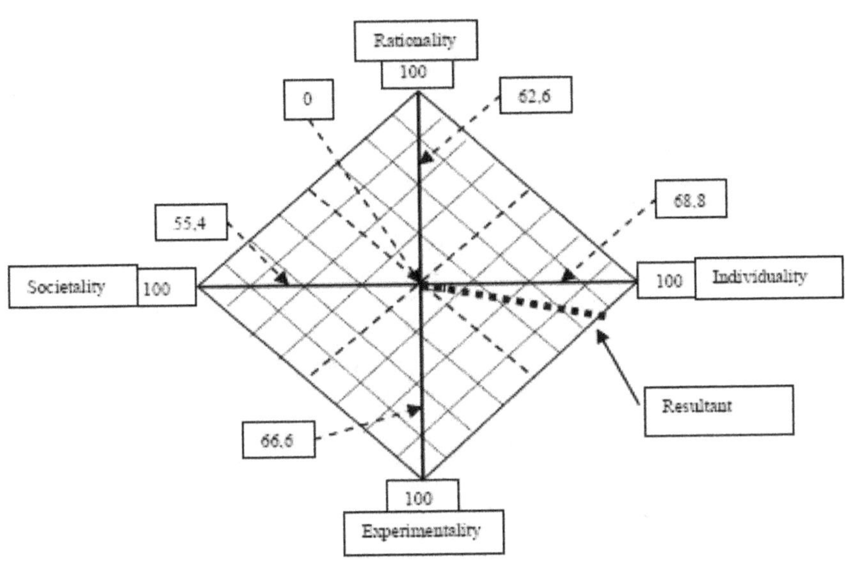

As we can see, the result indicates that the trend among the statistical population of respondents is in the "individualism-artism-moderantism" zone. This means that these are in a relativistic zone adapted to the modernism movement but their origin is primarily in the "holism-traditionalism-scientism" zone and then the "holism-populism-sophism" zone. In other words, our respondents are originally from a traditional society, but over time they moved to a complementary zone that best fits their new social environment.

Bibliography

- Akoun, André, *Dictionnaire de sociologie*, Paris, Le Robert, 1999.

- Alamdari, Kazem, *Why did Iran stay behind and the West progress?* (Chera Iran 'aghab mand va gharb pish raft?), Tehran, Nashr Towse'eh, 2001

- Antoine, Corinne, *Petit Larousse de la psychologie*, Paris, Larousse, 2005.

- Aron, Raymond, *Introduction à la philosophie de l'histoire, essai sur les limites de l'objectivité historique*, Paris, Gallimard, 1986.

- Beheshti, Seyyed Mohammad, *Knowledge with internal language* (Shenakht ba zaban e fetrat), Hezb e Jomhoury Eslamy.

- Berkeley, George, *Concerning the Principles of Human Knowledge*, Translated byYahya Mahdavi, Tehran, Université de Téhéran, 1966.

- Berkeley, George; *Three Dialogues between Hylas and Philonous*, translated by Manouchehr Bozorgmehr, Tehran, Université de Téhéran, 1976.

- Berthelot, Jean, *Les vertues de l'incertitude: le travail de l'analyse dans les sciences sociales*, Paris, PUF, 1996.

- Boudon, Raymond, *Dictionnaire critique de la sociologie*, Paris, PUF, 1986.

- Bourdieu, Pierre, *Raisons pratiques. Sur la théorie de l'action*, Paris, Seuil, 1984.

- Bozorgmehr, Manoutchehr, *The of logic's analysis* (falsafeh ye tahlil manteghy), Tehran, Entesharat e Karazmi, 1979.

- Crozier, Michel, *L'acteur et le système - Les contraintes de l'action collective*, Paris, Seuil, 1981.

- Dumont, *Louis, Essai sur l'individualisme - Une perspective anthropologique sur l'idéologie moderne*, Paris, Seuil, 1991.

- Dumont, Louis, *Homo oequalis*, Paris, Gallimard, 1977.

- Durant, William James, *History of Philosophy*, translated by Abbas Zaryab Khouiy, Tehran, Entesharat 'elmi va farhangi, 1994.

- Durant, William James, *Pleasures of Philosophy*, translated byAbbas Zaryab Khouiy, Tehran, Entesharat Amouzesh Enghelab eslami, 1990.

- Elster, Jon, *Foundations of Social Choice Theory*, Cambridge, Cambridge UP, 1990.

- Ensafpour, Gholamreza, *Iran and the Iranians* (Iran va Irani), Zowwar, 1984.

- Feshahi, Mohammad Reza, *Introduction to the development of thought in Middle-Age*, (moghadameh iy var seyr e tafakkor dar Ghoroun e vosta), Tehran, Entesharat e Goutenberg, 1975.

- Foroughi, Mohammad Ali, *Evolution of philosophy in Europe* (seyr e hekmat dar Oroupa), Tehran, Zowwar, 1965.

- Gaarder, Jostien, *Le monde de Sophie*, translated by hassan Kamshad, Tehran, Nashr Niloufar, 2002.

- Ghalamkaripour, Bijan, *L'univers mental des Iraniens*, Paris, L'Harmattan, 2012.

- Goffman, Erving, *Les Rites d'interaction*, Paris, Edition de Minuit, 1974.

- Grawitz, Madeleine, *Lexique des Sciences Sociales*, Paris, Dalloz, 1994.

- Ha'eri, Mehdi, *Theoretical research* (Kavosh-hay e 'aghl e nazari), Tehran, Amir Kabir, 1982.

- Hojjati Kermani, Ali, *Marxist dialectic method* (Metod e dialektik e marksisty), Tehran, Kanoun Nashr va Pajouhesh-hay e Eslami, ?.

- Ja'fari, Mohammad Taghi, *Knowledge and its dimensions from the point of view of the Quran* (shenakht va anva' va ab'ade ân az didgah e 'elmy va Qorân), Tehran, Daftar Nashr Farhang e Eslami, 1981.

- Jamalzadeh, Mohammad Ali, *Our Iranian habbits* (Kholghiyat e mâ iranian), Tehran, Entesharat Foroughi, 1966.

- Javadi Amoli, javad, *Epistemology in Quran* (shenakht shenasy dar Qorân), Qom, year ?.

- Kant, Emmanuel, *Critique de la raison pure*, translated byMir-shamsseddin Soltani, Tehran, Amir Kabir, 1983.

- Keyvan, B. *Knowledge and philosophical dialogue* (Shenakht va maghouleh ye falsafy), Tehran, Shabgir, 1978.

- Lalande, André, *Vocabulaire technique et critique de la philosophie*, Paris, PUF, 1985.

- Locke, john, *Essai sur l'entendement humain*, translated by Rezazadeh Shafagh, Tehran, Ketabforoushi dehkhoda, 1970.

- Mead, George Herbert, *L'Esprite, le soi et la société*, Paris, PUF, 1963.

- Mojtabavi, Seyyed jalaleddin, *Philosophy or the truth's research* (falsafeh ya pajouhesh haghighat), Tehran, Entesharat Hekmat, 1991.

- Mojtahedi, karim, *La philosophie critique de Kant* (Falsafeh ye naghghady Kant), Tehran, Nashr Homa, 1984.

- Motahari, Morteza, *The problem of knowledge* (mas'aleh ye shenakht), Sadra, 2008.

- Ogien, Albert, *Le vocabulaire de la sociologie de l'action*, Paris, Ellipses Edition Marketing, 2005.

- Parsons, Talcotte, *The Social System*, Tavistock, 1952.

- Pazargad, Baha'eddin, *Political schools* (Maktab-hay e siâssy), Tehran, Eghbal, 1965.

- Popper, Karl Raimund, *Objective knowledge*, translated by Ahmad Aram, Tehran, Entesharat 'elmi va farhangi, 1995.

- Popper, Karl Raimund, *The logic of scientific discovery*, translated by Ahmad Aram, Tehran, Entesharat Soroush, 1991.

- Quéré, Louis, *La théorie de l'action - Le sujet pratique en débat*, Paris, Edition du CNRS, 1993.

- Rabbani Golpaygani, Ali, *Introduction to theosophy* (madkhal va darâmad 'elm kalam), Tehran, Publication and year ?.

- Razavi, Morteza, *A view on sociology of knowledge* (Gozary bar jame'eh shenasy shenakht), Tehran, Entesharat Kayhan, 1992.

- Russell, Bertrand, *History of western philosophy*, translated by Najaf Daryabandari, Tehran, Ketab Parvaz, 1994.

- Russell, Bertrand, *Mysticism and Logic and Other Essays*, translated by Najaf Daryabandari, Tehran, Ketabhay Jibi, 1983.

- Russell, Bertrand, *The Problems of Philosophy*, translated by Ahmad Ordoubadi, Tehran, Kanoun Ma'refat, 1957.

- Sadr, Mohammad Bagher, *Our Philosophy* (falsafeh ye mâ), translated bySeyyed Mohammad hashan Mar'ashi Shoushtari, Tehran, Entesharat Sadr, 1972.

- Sadr, Mohammad Bagher, *Logical Foundations of Induction* (mabani e manteghi Esteghra'), translated by Seyyed Mohammad hashan Mar'ashi Shoushtari, Entesharat Sadr, 1972.

- Said, Edward W. *L'orientalisme, L'orient crée par l'Occident*, Paris, Seuil, 2003.

- Sajjadi, Seyyed Zia'eddin, *Thought and knowledge* (Seiry da andisheh va shenakht), Tehran, Nashr Pazang, 1988.

- Schütz, Alfred, *Le Chercheur et le quotidien - Phénoménologie des sciences sociales*, Belgique, Klincksieck, 1987.

- Shayegan, Dariush, *Religions and philosophy's schools in India* (Adyan va maktabhay e falsafy hend), Tehran, Amir Kabir, 1996.

- Simmel, Georg, *Sociologie et épistémologie*, Paris, PUF, 1981.

- Sobhani, Ja'far, *Knowledge in Islamic philosophy* (Shenakht dar falsafeh ye eslamy), Tehran, Entesharat Borhan, 1996.

- Sobhani, Ja'far, *Islamic Philosophy and Dialectic principles* (Falsafeh ye eslamy va ossoul e dialektik), Tehran, Entesharat Omid.

- Soroush, Abdelkarim, *What is Sciences? What is Philosophy?* ('elm chist ? falsafeh chist ?), Tehran, Payam Azadi, 1981.

- Spinoza, Baruch, *Traité de la réforme de l'entendement et de la meilleure voie à suivre pour parvenir à la vraie connaissance des choses*, Translated by Esmaiyl Sa'adat, Tehran, Nashr Markaz Daneshgahi, 1995.

- Tabatabaiy, Seyyed Mohammad Hossein, *The Principles of Philosophy and Method of Realism* (Ossoul e falsafeh va ravesh e realism), Tehran, Daftar Entesharat Eslami, 1978.

- Tourain, Alain, *Production de la société*, Paris, Seuil, 1973.

- Weber, Max, *Economie et société*, Paris, Plon, 1971.

- Weber, Max, *Essais sur la théorie de la science*, Paris, Presses Pocket, 1992.

- Zibakalam, Sadegh, *How Did We Become What We Are?* (Mâ chegouneh mâ shodim?), Tehran, Entesharat Rowzaneh, 1994.

www.ingramcontent.com/pod-product-compliance
Lightning Source LLC
Chambersburg PA
CBHW081845250726
48659CB00008B/2619